A Light at the End of the Tunnel

The Stories of Muslim Teens

A collection of short stories written by
Sumaiya Beshir and other Muslim teens

COMPILED BY SUMAIYA BESHIR

amana publications

First Edition
2007A.C./1428A.H.

Copyright © 2007 A.C./1428 A.H.
amana publications
10710 Tucker Street
Beltsville, MD 20705-2223 USA
Tel: (301) 595-5999
Fax: (301) 595-5888

Email: amana@igprinting.com
Website: amana-publications.com

Library of Congress Cataloging-in-Publication Data

A light at the end of the tunnel : the stories of Muslim teens
/ compiled by Sumaiya Beshir. – 1st ed.
    p. cm.
 ISBN 978-1-59008-050-4
1. Group identity–United States. 2. Muslim youth–United
States. I. Beshir, Sumaiya.

HN59.2.L536 2007
305.235088'297–dc22

2007042045

Printed in the United States of America by
International Graphics, 10710 Tucker Street
Beltsville, MD 20705-2223
Tel: (301) 595-5999
Fax: (301) 595-5888

Acknowledgements

Bismillah Alrahman Alraheem
[In the name of Allah, the most gracious, the most merciful]

All praise is to Allah the most high, the beneficent, the merciful.

The word acknowledgement does not do justice to express how greatly the following people have contributed to this collection of short stories. My dear mother and father, as always, helped guide me through this process and were with me every step of the way. But most of all, they nurtured in me the love of expression through words. Thank you for your endless support and encouragement and for all the time you spent on this. A few years ago, I would never have imagined that so much could be accomplished over the telephone (so I guess a thank you to Alexander Graham Bell is in order here too!).

And to my dear husband, thank you for your support, your patience, and your exceptional QA skills that helped expose all sorts of typos in the knick of time. To my dear sister Noha (also known as the comma, and now quotations queen), thank you for all your diligent work during the final edit of this book.

Thank you to all the fellow writers who contributed to this book. May Allah *subhanahu wa ta'ala* reward you for every letter you wrote.

And to the reader, thank you for taking the time to read this. May it be at least a small beam of light in dark times.

Contributors

I would like to sincerely thank the following people
for their priceless contribution to this book:

Aseel Abudayya
Hossam Amin
Amanie Antar
Noha Beshir
Amira Elghawaby
Lena Hassan
Tessa Santoni

Table of Contents

Introduction and the Magic P

Perspective is not something you can buy. You can't pick it up in the local supermarket, nor will you find it at the department store for half price on Boxing Day. You have to acquire it, often through living certain experiences—certain difficult experiences.

The ironic thing about perspective is that you don't know you're missing it until you have it. And when you do finally get it, it's like a light bulb went on in your head, and suddenly, you see the whole world in a different way. When I look back at high school days now, not too long ago from when I eagerly marched across the stage and gladly welcomed my diploma, I realize that throughout most of that time, the majority of us were lacking perspective. And it was this lack of something so integral to our view of life that caused us the adolescent grief our society insists is all too normal. I wouldn't say all teenagers are naïve, but definitely impressionable. We try a little too hard to please everyone in life. And too often, we think high school is life. But high school isn't life; it's a stage, a passing stage. You learn that with perspective. It is my hope that the stories contained in this book can help us all gain a little more of this much needed antidote, can help us get a clearer handle on this magic P. I leave you now with stories and memories, because eventually, that is all we will have of each other.

Sincerely,
Sumaiya Beshir

Words

Words can bounce off walls
Unheard, unacknowledged, or just plain ignored
Words can fly in one ear and out the other
Deflecting distracted eyes that bound around the room as you talk
Words can be erased, torn into pieces, ripped apart
Often misconstrued or just misunderstood
Words can sting you, eat at you, keep you lying awake at night
And in the morning, and then in the afternoon
Words are letters strung together to create a meaning that may or may
not get across what you originally intended it to
Words are symbols of a message you are trying to convey
But symbols are often indirect, convoluted
In the end words are only words no matter how you put them,
   arrange them, or voice them
But prayers…
Prayers rise to the heavens where they are awaited,
   acknowledged and accounted for
Prayers cannot be misconstrued or misunderstood
For He who hears them understands their meaning
   more deeply then he who speaks them
Prayers originate in the heart
And even when they don't roll off the tongue
Prayers ascend to high places that are only seen in dreams
Prayers are always heard, even when left unspoken
Prayers are words immortalized

The Identity Trap

Nine years since the day I first entered my high school as a grade nine student, after finishing my secondary education, starting and completing a university degree in neuroscience, and beginning my life as a young Muslim woman in the Canadian workforce, after forgetting the names of most of my teachers, the titles of most of my textbooks, and the faces of most of my peers, I can still remember my friend Elizabeth's outfit on the first day of school.

It was the Tuesday after Labour Day, a cool fall morning at 8:15 when the bell first rang and we were ushered into Ms. Bernard's class for the first time. The looks on our faces were a blend of fear, excitement, and lack of sleep, each person looking to find a chair in the maze of tables, to seat themselves somewhere important, as close to the students in designer labels as possible–without looking desperate–and as far from the fat boy with glasses as possible–without looking shallow.

Because I hesitated too long, because I looked for my seat, tried to analyze the right place to sit instead of finding a place as quickly as I could, I ended up at an entirely forgettable table, not cool or uncool, just there with the other kids who belonged somewhere in the middle of the high school continuum of importance. Maybe I could have been considered the "freak" at my table. After all, I was the only person in the classroom, probably the only person in the whole school, wearing a headscarf. But I'd been wearing it for three years, and had gotten over the obvious attention it brought me, the arrow it pointed my way.

Elizabeth was sitting two tables away in the front of the room, even her position signifying, right from the start, that she mattered, that she was ahead, that people should look her way. I quietly chided myself for being just another person at one of the middle tables, average, forgettable. She was wearing a purple mini-skirt and a black, lacey t-shirt, with a low neckline, her reddish-blondish hair falling onto her shoulders, bangs just long enough that she would need to constantly brush them out of her eyes. Her make up was super-model perfect. Her sandals had pointy heels.

I can't remember for sure what I was wearing that day, but my typical grade nine outfit consisted of baggy jeans and a long-sleeved t-shirt or sweatshirt to go with my white headscarf and running shoes. No makeup. No nail polish. No bangs in the eyes. I believed in this, hadn't been forced into wearing hijab by my parents, but there was always that little part of me who would see a girl like Elizabeth and think, "if only I could look that good…"

The rest of the first day is a blur in my mind, who met who, where we ate, what we learned. It was the following weeks that made their stamp on the next four years of my life, those first few weeks of high school, when you're trying to figure out where you fit, whether to stay in your junior-high cliques or to meet new people, carve out a new identity, become someone different. In my head I entered high school with the goal to be a different Kareema than the one I'd been in junior high. The junior high Kareema had been the smartest girl in the class, the one who'd write the answers on the board at the teacher's request during math class, the one with her work done first, but still sitting quietly. Junior-high Kareema sang in the choir. She didn't play on any of the school's sports teams. She didn't have leads in school plays. She didn't know the popular kids, or rather they didn't know her.

My plan was to make high school Kareema an improvement. To be picked early on in gym class. To play on the sports teams. To be more than "the smart girl". I wanted to be the witty girl. The creative girl. And—just a little bit—I wanted to be the pretty girl.

So over those first few weeks, I sat near Elizabeth in our shared classes, and within a month, her and I had become part of the same group of friends, a group that sat together, ate lunch together, walked together from class to class, traded jokes and whispers. There were four of us in the core group: Elizabeth, Brenda, Christianne, and I. Of course, there were others like Mindy, Tamara, Juliana, and Kim who shifted in and out of the various circles, including ours.

I sometimes wonder if my three friends and I sought each other out because we were really the best friends for each other, or because each of our outward identities didn't threaten anyone else's. Elizabeth (who was only called Elizabeth by the teachers, everyone else called her Lizzie) was our requisite pretty girl. She was the one whose outfits were diligently complimented every morning, whose hairdo was jealously pointed too, whose makeup was marveled over. I was the smart one, the one who was asked for the answers to last night's homework, the one who was turned to for explanations about trigonometry and chemical equations. Christianne was the creative one. We listened to her poems, read the books she recommended and paid attention to the way she decorated her locker. Brenda was our two-in-one witty-slash-sporty girl. She played football, soccer, and rugby. She joked about the teachers. She made faces about everything. She made impressions of the principal and school president. Her job was to make us laugh and our job was to laugh.

Even our names said something about our chosen or imposed identities. Lizzie's name was fun and light and soft to say. It sounded exactly like the way she looked, like the way she walked, like the way she smiled. There was a sparkle to it, a certain radiance.

Christianne's name was who she wanted to become: the sophisticated artist. All through grade school and junior-high, Christianne had been the sporty girl, and all her friends and family had called her Chris. I remember a few of the other kids in our school who'd been in junior-high with her, a girl named Nancy who kept calling her Chris, and Christianne would correct her with an exasperated look in her eyes, a "that was then" look, before she turned back to her latest creative endeavor. Christianne's name had a European sound to it, which added to the mystery, the classiness of it to our Canadian ears. We loved the way it rolled off our tongues, the way it made us feel like we were characters in a foreign film.

Brenda was either called Brenda or just "Bren" if we needed to shorten it. Tough, strong, tomboyish and easy to laugh along with. It fit her identity perfectly, the sporty, funny girl.

Me, I was just Kareema. Simple, practical Kareema, no short or long versions, no endearing nicknames. I kept trying to think of a change in my name that would give my identity more flair but nothing worked. It fit perfectly with being the practical girl, the smart girl.

Still, I wanted to be more than the smart, practical, boring girl, and grade nine was the only chance I had at a new beginning, the only chance to cement myself in a different role than the same old one I'd been playing for two years. I had to do something now before I was stuck like this for another four years, so when Bren showed up at lunch one afternoon and said she was trying out for the junior tennis team, and asked if anyone wanted to go with her, I knew I had to do it. All it took was one look around me and I was convinced: there I was, with Christianne on one side of me, in a tie-dyed peasant dress, writing a poem, and Lizzie on the other side, re-applying her 'Won't Kiss Off' Cover-Girl lipstick, and waterproof mascara. Who was I kidding? These girls had the market covered on creative and pretty. At least there was more than one available opening for sporty. I had to take it.

Tennis try-outs were after school in mid-October and would last a week before the team was picked, but it became clear on day one that I would make the team. Not because I could serve like a pro, or volley very well, not because my forehand or backhand was good, not because I could rally and run and my competitive spirit was something to be reckoned with, but because there were exactly the same number of spots on the team as there were people trying out. I was partially insulted: I wanted to make it on my own merits, to be good enough that with 30 other people fighting for my spot, I would still beat them out, but that was in my dream-world. In reality, I held my breath and prayed that no one else would try out for the rest of the week so I could make the team.

And my prayers were answered. It felt so good for the two weeks before our first tournament to casually mention to everyone I saw that I was on the tennis team–leaving out of course the part about *how* I'd made it. I carried my tennis racket to and from every afternoon class, telling myself that there was no time after the final bell rang to get it from my locker–which was all the way in the North end of the school on the second floor–before I had to be at the Gym–which was all the way in the South end of the school on the first floor–for warm up. Half the time after class, I would end up walking back to the lockers with Bren anyway, since she insisted on leaving her racket upstairs, and we'd rush back down the hall and through the stairwells on a mission not to be late, huffing for air by the time we arrived at the gym doors.

My first tennis tournament was a rude awakening: I lost every match in the round-robin and failed to make the play-offs, so I spent the rest of the day playing Bren's cheerleader-slash-water-girl, refilling her bottle and trying to give her tips on where to stand and how far to hit. I had one more tournament a week later, which I also lost every match at, before tennis season, and my first attempt at sportiness, was over. It's hard to describe now, so many years later, how difficult it was to answer people when they asked me how I'd done. A sense of resentment would pour over me as I tried to answer the questions lightly, explain away how tough most of my opponents had been, move quickly on to another topic. Strangely, it was always easiest to bring up some schoolwork to change the subject, which would lead my friends to ask me for help in the math or science homework, help I would have no problem giving, and slowly my pride would return as I explained the different variables of the quadratic equation with confidence.

I was determined not to abandon my sporty image completely, and for the rest of the year, I continued to go with Bren to the school's weight room at lunch once or twice a week, to learn the lingo, find out once and for all what the difference was between a barbell and a dumbbell, at least be recognized by the jocks at school as more than just a face, but a name. Still, as we returned again and again, I found I lost interest after ten minutes of weightlifting, didn't really want to spend my entire, precious lunch hour doing something I didn't even like that much, and by the end of the year, I'd stopped going altogether.

Grade ten was marked by my attempts to try out my creative side, to try again to break out of the 'smart girl' role I hadn't managed to leave behind in my first year of high school. This meant I had to find an artsy area where I could stand out, and I spent some time considering my options before I picked one category. In music, I wasn't going to play any instruments, since they were all Islamically questionable, and I definitely wasn't going to sing on my own. Joining the choir, like I had in junior-high, was out of the question even though I was confident I had the voice for it. Choir was too typical, too boring, too goodie-goodie. I wanted to be artistic to stand out, not to be one random head in a group of fifty. In drama, again, my options were limited. If I took a drama class, I was at the teacher's mercy if anything inappropriate happened. And there were almost always girl-boy interactions, so drama was a write-off. So I was down to creative writing or drawing. I'd always enjoyed both English and Art class, and I'd always been good at both, so here I could just pick the one I wanted to try out more.

I decided to go with writing when our English teacher asked if anyone was interested in submitting poetry on a monthly basis to the school paper. There would be my poem, with my name beside it in the paper for all 1500 students of our school to see. Christianne and I both decided to offer our names and the teacher nodded at us. Our first deadline was a week away. I was excited. I spent my bus rides to and from school scribbling down random half-poems, hoping they'd fit together brilliantly, waiting for that one amazing inspiration. I flipped through old journals I'd kept for years, flipped through poems I'd handed in as homework assignments in English class, tried to find the perfect one to submit. I dreamt poetry, breathed poetry, thought poetry for a week, the way I had with tennis just the year before. Christianne and I edited each other's offerings at lunchtime, reviewed each and every word the other had written, crossed out the's and a's, re-arranged stanzas and line-breaks. Bren and Lizzie were as supportive as they could be, though for the most part, Bren was off at this year's tennis try-outs during lunch, while Lizzie would take turns admiring our poems and we would take turns admiring the Tommy-Girl t-shirt her latest boyfriend had bought for her.

I finally settled on a poem at the end of the week and dropped it into the paper's submission slot an hour before the deadline, on my way out of the school on Friday afternoon. The paper would be out the next Thursday morning, and for those five days in between I held my breath and hoped and prayed and hoped some more. What if they got so many submissions that they decided not to include mine? What if the poem I'd spent hours and hours writing and crafting was actually not that good? What if Christianne's poem made it and mine didn't? I knew I could simply ask the editor of the paper if the poem was in or not, but that seemed so desperate, and I wanted to look cool about the whole thing, as though I had my writing published all the time, as though it wasn't a big deal or not whether my poem was in there. But it was a big deal.

All through the next week, Christianne and I danced around the subject without ever directly bringing it up. We went to the library and checked out poetry books, we were always reading. In place of the tennis racket that had seemed an extension of my arm the year before, I now had a trusty copy of Michael Ondaatje's latest and greatest works in hand everywhere I went. It was a completely different look than the racket gave me. The racket had been this loud appendage, and with it, I'd become louder. Now, with my book, I needed to become quiet to match. Quiet and calm, but sophisticated. I hoped it fit. I hoped I fit.

On Thursday morning, I arrived at school an extra fifteen minutes early and found a stack of the papers in the lobby. I grabbed two copies, flipped through as quickly as I could manage, trying to find my poem. There it was on page eight, in the top left corner, exactly as I had submitted it except for one minor glitch: my last name had been misspelled. Instead of *Night Owls by Kareema Waleed*, the paper glared back with *Night Owls by Kareema Waleeed*. Who cares, I told myself. It was a typo. Everyone knew nothing was ever spelled with three 'e's in a row. I breathed in deeply and let out a small squeal of joy, reading over my poem slowly, verifying to myself again that it was good, that I deserved to be there. Satisfied, I looked over the page to ensure that Christianne's poem had also made it, and there it was, on the right side of the same page, perfectly typed. We were the only Grade ten poems in the paper! I picked up another two copies to give to Lizzie and Bren, shook my head, and put them back down. Let them get the paper themselves when they came. It didn't look as desperate that way.

When I got to our lockers, I handed Christianne her copy and gave a big smile. We re-read each other's poems, one more time (as if we didn't already have them memorized), and smiled our congratulations. As we prepared to go to class, I folded my paper open to page eight and left the top sticking out of my schoolbag, so *Night Owls, by Kareema Waleeed* would show from the top. For the rest of the day, each time I heard my name called out, I would silently hold my breath, waiting for a comment on the poem. But most of my class-mates hadn't seen the paper. Most of them were asking me if I knew how to do Exercise number four in Math class, or what my results had been for the science lab. The artsy group was small, I discovered, and there was very little spotlight associated with its successes.

I submitted a second poem the next month, and a third in November, and much to my joy, both were printed. But as we approached finals for the semester, I found I had no time to write any-thing worthy of school paper publication. The problem had less to do with studying and more to do with all the promises I'd made of help-ing other people study. In the two weeks before final exams in December, I had booked myself nearly solid: two days of the week after school, I was helping Christianne, Brenda, and a few other girls with the last three math units; another day I had promised to study history with Lizzie and Mindy. And then there was my promise, which would take at least three different sessions, to Tamara and Kim to explain all the chemistry experiments we'd done in science class. I tried working on my December poem on my bus rides home, but suddenly found I couldn't concentrate over my schoolmates' voices and the chill of the wind at each stop.

"It's not fair," I complained to my mother one night as the deadline for submissions approached. "I would have had more than enough time to do my own studying and write the poem if I wasn't doing all this extra studying too. I mean, I already understand trig, and it's not that hard, but I swear we spent 45 minutes going over it in the library after school today, and I still don't think Brenda gets it!"

My mother, who was standing at the kitchen counter, loading the dishwasher as I ate my belated dinner at the table, stopped and looked at me. I spooned another mouthful of pasta into my mouth and chewed slowly, avoiding her gaze, knowing I'd crossed the 'complain-ing' line into the 'inappropriate complaining' zone somehow. "Kareema," she said quietly, and rinsed her hands off, "let's think a little bit about what you just said." I watched her walk over and sit next to me at the table, folding her hands on the surface. "You're angry because you haven't had time to write a poem for the school paper, right?"

I nodded.

"Did you promise your friends you would help them study?"

I nodded again, but quickly saw my chance to defend myself, "I did, but I didn't think it would take so much time."

"Why do you want that poem in the paper so much?"

"I don't know, I just… I've had one in every issue this year."

"Do you feel you're behind on your own studying because of the time you're spending helping them to study?"

I shook my head.

"I want to tell you a *hadeeth*, Kareema, and I want you to focus on the meaning. The Prophet, Peace be Upon Him, said, '*Khayrunnassi anfa'ahum linnass*'."

I stared at my plate blankly as my mother pushed on.

"It means, 'the best of you is the one that is most helpful to others'. There's nothing wrong with wanting to publish your writing, but you made your friends a promise, and if you miscalculated how much time it would take to keep that promise, you shouldn't resent them for it. Think how many good deeds you can get by helping them study, if you have the right intentions. And there's another thing, honey."

She reached for my hand, waiting for me to meet her gaze over my now-cold pasta. Reluctantly, I looked up, afraid she'd have disappointment all over her face. She was smiling kindly instead.

"Allah *subhana wa ta'ala* gives different people different blessings. He's blessed you with a lot of intelligence, and that's something you have to be proud of, and to use properly. Don't judge other people because sometimes they don't understand things as quickly as you do, or all the good deeds you've gotten for helping them are erased by bad deeds you'll get for judging them." She gave me a kiss on my forehead and stood back up to finish loading the dishwasher. "Now, do you want to tell me about the rest of your day?"

For two days after our conversation, I quietly looked through my old writing for a poem I could use. I was determined to still have something published in the December issue, but I knew my mother was right, and that I couldn't break a promise I'd made to help other people study, because now they were depending on my help. My search was futile: everything I'd written in ninth grade, just a year before, seemed childish, amateur, or over-exaggerated. I went through the stuff I'd written for English throughout the current school term, but found each poem either too boring, or too obviously a homework assignment, and I couldn't imagine my entire class knowing I had submitted my homework to be published in the paper. How goodie-two shoes could that be? In the end, I gave up, and the December paper was published with only Christianne's poem representing the tenth grade, but no one really seemed to notice my missing piece but me.

On the first day of our second semester, the day we got our first term report cards, Brenda skipped up to me at our lockers as lunch hour was beginning.

"Hey, genius," she grinned, smacking me playfully on the back.

"How'd you do? Anything below a hundred percent?"

"Haha Bren, are you kidding me? How about 'everything' below a hundred percent."

"No, seriously Kareema, thanks a billion for helping me with math. Guess what I got?" She looked beyond proud as she pulled her report card out of her backpack. She had rolled it into a scroll, and now unrolled it for my benefit.

"82! Way to go Bren!" I pushed my bag into my locker and closed it before she asked to see my report card. I was afraid she'd bring up my math grade, and I would have felt embarrassed, almost guilty to tell her I'd gotten 97% without really trying all that hard. Then I remembered the extra practice sessions we'd spent on the court last year after I'd 'made' the tennis team, how Brenda had spent ages with me after training had officially ended, trying to teach me how to properly return the ball with my backhand. My mother's words flushed through me, 'Allah blesses everyone with different things'. "It's one for one," I said, as I unwrapped my tuna sandwich. "We're even now. You help me with tennis, I help you with math."

"It's too bad you're not taking gym again this term," she replied, "I'd help you some more with your serve if you were."

"Oh, I think my tennis days are behind me, Bren. Sometimes you've gotta quit while you're ahead."

I would only be seeing Brenda one class a day that term, and that was in Social Studies, which the four of us had signed up for together. Otherwise, I had one more class with Christianne and one more class with Lizzie. With Christianne, I was taking Canadian Literature, with Lizzie, we'd decided to get a head start and take grade 11 Chemistry a year early. I had been working my excitement up over Literature class from the end of last term, borrowing two Margaret Atwood novels from Christianne over the holidays and promising to have them read by the time classes started. I imagined myself holed up in my room, a young writer, unable to fall asleep at night with her nightlight on, a pen tucked in behind my ear and my eyes pouring over the books as I devoured the words page by page. Instead, by the first day of class, I had barely managed to get through half of one of them. I had spent my holiday skating outside without my younger brothers and going to all the youth halaqas I didn't have time for during the school term.

Canadian Literature was our third period, and as we walked to the classroom, Christianne passed me a paper. "It's my poem for January," she announced, and I nodded quickly, faking my excitement at her scribbled handwriting. How was it she was able to come up with these poems so quickly? How did she manage to make a few lines about the snow on the pavement sound so deep, so profound?

"It's nice," I said. "I like the line about the frozen water."

"Did you read the novels I lent you?"

"I got started, but I didn't really have time to finish them."

"Have you started on your poem?"

"To be honest, I'm not sure I'm going to hand in anything this month. I mean, I'm not sure how hard grade 11 chemistry will be, so..." I let my voice trail off. I wasn't sure why I'd signed up for this class to begin with, why I'd thought I would love a course about a bunch of old writers who went on and on about winter and snow and the Prairies and the Maritimes so much.

I daydreamed through Literature until the bell went for Chemistry, and hurried out to meet Lizzie in the science hallway by the lab, where our class was waiting for the third period science class to vacate the room. I found her standing with Jason Sherman, her new boyfriend, who was actually a twelfth grader, giggling as he rolled his eyes about something and whispered loudly into her ear. His arm was wrapped around her tiny waist. Even in the January weather, a tiny part of her toned midriff showed.

"Hey Lizzie," I called out, as I walked up to them, "hey Jason."

Jason nodded at me absentmindedly and turned back to Lizzie. "I gotta go to Algebra," he said, "I'll meet you after school at the bus stop."

I watched Lizzie watch Jason walk away to catch up with a few other twelfth grade boys, and then she turned to look at me. "He got me this awesome perfume for Christmas. It smells sooooo good," she said, as the lab door finally opened and our class went in.

"He sounds really sweet," I said, looking for something to say back to her.

"He is," she answered, "and he's gorgeous too."

Aside from Lizzie and I, only two other tenth graders were in the Chemistry class. Everyone else was either in the eleventh or twelfth grade. We sat on benches, three to a bench. I was seated next to Lizzie, and on her other side, our third bench mate was an eleventh grader named Matt, who was tall and thin with longish hair and wore baggy jeans and an earring in his left ear. As our teacher, Mr. Ray, passed out our lab manuals and textbooks, it was clear that Matt was a lot more interested in Lizzie than he was in chemistry. Twice during the first ten minutes, he poked her in the ribs over her tight pink sweatshirt. Both times, she giggled quietly and pretended to ignore him. The third time, she looked his way and whispered, "what?"

"Do you have a sharpener?" I heard him ask.

Lizzie nodded and reached for her pencil case.

"Here, sharpen my pencil," he ordered and handed it to her, his hand brushing over hers a few seconds longer than necessary. My face burned as I scribbled Mr. Ray's instructions into my notebook. Lizzie had a boyfriend already, but there was no denying her and Matt would look good together. Then again, in her pink hoodie and a little of her waist showing, Lizzie looked good with just about anyone.

As the chemistry lesson continued, I found myself calculating the number of boyfriends Lizzie had had in the year and a half since high school had started. Five, as far as I could remember, and that didn't include the times in between boyfriends, when she went out with more than one guy until she decided who she would date next. Lizzie almost always went out with someone in an older grade, the exception to this being a guy named Andrew at the beginning of the year who had failed tenth grade. I stole a quick glance over at my friend, re-examining her reddish-blondish hair, her pink sweatshirt and skintight jeans. She was wearing a soft pink shade of lipstick, thick eye shadow and loads of mascara. I knew from accompanying her to the washroom how much cover-up went into hiding the small pimples on her chin and forehead. I brushed a hand over my own forehead, felt for the hard bumps along my skin, imagined them protruding from my face. Matt was a good-looking guy, really good-looking actually, but he would never have taken a second look at me for anything but an experiment answer with my zitty face and my plain, baggy jeans. Lizzie and I weren't really all that different, I found myself thinking. We were both good at math and science, weren't we? And we were both pretty. She was just a lot prettier. But with a little bit of work, I could look–maybe–almost as good as she did. *It's haraam*–I told myself–*haraam and wrong and who cares whether Matt likes you*– banishing the thought of a tighter pair of pants, a shorter sweatshirt, but the idea just wouldn't go away.

For the next two weeks, I squirmed through chemistry, watching Matt and Lizzie flirt through the lesson and the lab, doing the bulk of the work for our group during experiments while he pulled at her hair and went through her pencil case and she giggled at his antics. No one seemed to notice that they fooled around all period while I worked like crazy. No one seemed to notice me, period. After class, I would go with Lizzie to the washroom, watch as she re-applied her lip-liner, lipstick, and lip gloss, as she went over her face with the cover up and sprayed perfume on her wrists before going to meet Jason by the bus stop. By the time we got to our lockers, Christianne and Brenda, having tired of waiting for us, would be gone for their own bus stops or about to leave.

I let the January poetry deadline pass me without submitting any-thing. I was bored in Canadian Literature, watching Christianne answer questions and realizing that she really enjoyed this, that she really wanted to be a writer like the people who's stories we were studying. The truth was, of course, that I wasn't writer material, just like I hadn't been tennis material. I was more like Lizzie than I was like either of my other two friends, and there wasn't anything wrong with admitting that, or acting on it.

I waited until we were alone in the girls' washroom one day after school, as Lizzie was fixing her makeup, to start acting on it. Lizzie was wearing a spaghetti strap tank top and a short green skirt, her tight, zip-on hoodie sticking out of the top of her schoolbag. Meanwhile, I was wearing a pair of loose black pants and a long, loose red button-up with my usual white scarf. "Hey Liz," I asked casually.

"Uh-huh," she answered, her mouth curled into a perfect 'O' as she ran the tube of lip-gloss over her lips.

"Do you mind if I borrow that hoodie tomorrow?" I pointed to her school bag.

"Oh that? Not at all. Go for it. You can take it home tonight if you want."

"Cool," I said, reaching into her bag and taking out the sweatshirt. It was tiny. I had no idea how I'd fit into it, let alone get out of the house with it on.

"Oh," I added, trying to sound casual, "I got some of that Cover Girl lipstick you said you found on sale at the pharmacy yesterday, but I wanted your opinion on it, since you're the make up queen." My heart was pumping so loud, I was sure she could hear it. "Can I meet you in the morning before class and maybe you can tell me if it's the right shade on my skin or not?"

Lizzie looked pleasantly surprised and her face brightened up. "Sure Kareema, sounds great. We'll do our makeup together tomorrow morning."

I got to school early the next day in my favourite gray jeans and a button up I didn't plan on wearing for very long, ran to the girls' washroom with my coat still on, and changed out of my shirt and into Lizzie's hoodie in a stall. When I came out and confronted myself in the mirror, I was half excited, half disgusted. The hoodie didn't look right on me, what with my scarf ruining the outfit, and my jeans were still way too loose to go with it. It actually made me look a little fat. I took a deep breath and sucked my stomach in, but there was no getting rid of my bulge.

I could still change; no one but Lizzie knew I'd wanted to borrow the hoodie in the first place. I stood in front of the mirror for what seemed like forever, considering my options, when the door opened and two of the girls from my social studies class came in. Too late.

A minute later, Lizzie was standing beside me at the counter, showing me how to apply the dark red lipstick to my mouth. When we were done, she handed me her eyeliner, mascara, and cover-up while she coloured her own lips a deep purple. I looked at the two of us, standing there side by side. She looked great, I thought, and I looked, well, ridiculous.

"Oh my God," she squealed, as she put her make up bag into her schoolbag and turned to look at me. "You look gorgeous! You should wear red lipstick more often, Kareema. It totally goes with your olive skin tone." Maybe she was right, I thought. Maybe I just had to get used to it.

And so my love affair with make up began. Each morning, I would paint my face in the washroom with Lizzie, and each night, after she left for the bus stop to meet Jason, I'd go back in to the school and scrub my face clean before I caught the next bus home. I told my mother the reason I was coming home later was that Lizzie and I were studying Chemistry for a half hour every night in the library after school, that it really was harder than we had expected. She believed me, and it drove me crazy with guilt how she looked at me proudly, pleased that I'd made the extra effort to take the course a year early, and that I was now making the extra effort to do as well as I could.

I got good at applying lipstick and mascara, learned the right amount of cover up and eyeliner to put on so that my face wouldn't look overdone, but there would still be an effect. As for the tighter shirts, after that first day, I couldn't bring myself to borrow more of Lizzie's clothes. I just felt wrong in them, and I didn't know if it was because I knew they were completely against *hijab*, or because I felt so much fatter when I was wearing them. Eventually, I decided I would need to lose some weight, and I decided I would start cutting down on breads and dessert until I looked better. During one of our morning makeup sessions, as I was finishing up my mascara, Lizzie took a long look at me and shook her head. "Kareema, you have such beautiful, thick black hair. Are you sure you wanna hide it all? I mean, I'd totally die for your hair."

She held up her own carefully dyed locks as though they were plain and boring next to my unruly curls. "I don't know, Liz," I answered, taking a deep breath. "I mean, I can't just take off my *hijab*, you know?"

"Not even just at school?" she pressed on.

Wrong Wrong WRONG! A voice in my head shouted, but I turned its volume down and stared into the washroom mirror, trying to figure out what to say to my beautiful friend. "Well, maybe I wouldn't mind showing a little of my bangs," I said, thinking I'd found the perfect compromise, and I reached my hand in under my scarf, loosening some of my hair from a barrette and pulling it down over my forehead.

"You'll need some hairspray to hold it in place," she told me, reaching into her bag for her bottle.

But even with my bangs showing and the cover up hiding the pimples on my face, I seemed to leave no lasting impression on Matt in chemistry class beyond that of science whiz-kid. I finally figured I must have been wrong about being pretty. Really, no amount of make up would make me look as good as Lizzie. It was the fat, I concluded. The fat and the darker skin and wild, messy hair. Wearing loose clothing all these years had made me lazy, and now I would have to make up for all the flab I'd let myself accumulate. As midterms rolled around in April, and my mom made my favourite comfort food to help me study, I thanked her politely and let the plates go untouched on my desk while I drank more and more coffee instead. I started weighing myself each morning in the washroom as I got ready for school, started buying bottle after bottle of hair mousse with my allowance and dumping it in my hair, all to tame that bit of bang that showed from the front of my scarf each day, as if that bit of bang being straight would be my most glorious victory, would reshape me into the pretty girl I longed to be.

Christianne, Brenda, Lizzie and I decided to study in the library after school as midterms approached. We had just finished a difficult unit in Chemistry, and try as I might, I couldn't wrap my head around it. As we sat in the library the day before the Chemistry exam, I was starting to panic, because in class, Lizzie had complained loudly to Matt and I that she was totally lost, and I didn't know who else to ask about it.

"Okay girls, quiz time," said Brenda, flipping through her Social Studies text book, "what's the percentage of families in North America where the kids go to college or university after high school?"

"I wish I cared," I said, tapping my pencil on my Chemistry notebook listlessly. "If I can't figure out this precipitation thing, I'm gonna fail this midterm."

"Kareema, you never fail anything," said Christianne, "you'll get like 80%, worst case. It'll be fine."

"No, really, it won't be. I'm lost. L-O-S-T," I told them.

"What part don't you get," Lizzie asked me, "maybe I can explain it to you."

"You can't. You already said in class you didn't get it."

"I know," she replied quietly. "I was just kidding."

I looked at her, puzzled for a moment, and then slid my notebook over in front of her . "Here, can you figure out how to find out the concentration where the compound precipitates?"

Lizzie started to re-explain Mr. Ray's lesson patiently. I watched, at first in disbelief that she had pretended not to understand in class, and then just relieved that someone was finally explaining it to me and I would understand it before the midterm. But that night, lying at home in bed trying to fall asleep, Lizzie's charade came back to me.

"This makes no sense at all," Matt had said, as Mr. Ray finished his explanation on precipitation by the blackboard. "I swear, the old man's on drugs."

Lizzie had flicked her hair back with one hand, shaken her head, and looked with her big brown eyes straight at Matt. "I totally don't get it either. I'm beyond confused." She had lied. Just so he wouldn't think she'd understood something he didn't.Even though she hadn't needed to, even though he hadn't even asked if she'd gotten it. She had lied. The more I thought about it, the more it bothered me, and quite suddenly it dawned on me that in Chemistry class, Lizzie rarely spoke without giggling, rarely gave an answer or raised her hand to participate though I knew she knew all the answers. Then I thought of the way she acted in every class we had been in with a cute boy, and it was the same. She had always pretended she was stupid, or bored, in every subject we had been in together since high school had started. But I knew for a fact that she wasn't stupid, knew that Lizzie almost always got 90's, especially in her math and science courses. For some reason though, she'd decided she had to hide it.

That night in bed, as I tossed and turned, my mind alternating between all the formulas I needed to know for our midterm and Lizzie's bizarre actions, I solved the most complicated formula of all, the formula that determined Lizzie's behaviour: just as two chemical compounds often repelled each other, the personas of the pretty girl and the smart girl were in complete contradiction. Before high school had started, Lizzie had found herself with the ingredients for both, and recognizing the incompatibility, she had had to make a choice, and she had chosen. No one asked her for answers on the night before's homework; no one wanted her to explain the quadratic equation or the periodic table or the rules of trigonometry. These were questions that couldn't be asked of a girl who wore pink lipstick and short skirts and constantly giggled, questions that couldn't be asked of a girl who was never without a boyfriend, of a girl whose defining characteristic was that she was pretty; and she had wanted the pink lipstick and the boyfriends more, and so she hid the other half of herself.

But was she right? Was it not possible that I could be smart and pretty? Couldn't I still be both, or was it too late for me? Could I not be pretty because everyone already knew that I was smart, or was it simply that I didn't have what it took to be pretty? I felt my eyes well up at the injustice of it all, at how being a certain colour, looking a certain way seemed to be all that mattered and I could do nothing about it, at how little I felt wanted and valued by my classmates. I thought as I lay there about how no one ever rushed to sit beside me during lunch hour, only during class, how they wouldn't even have missed me if they could replace me with a computer to spit out their answers.

I fell asleep the night before that midterm fitfully, my eyes wet and my mind heavy and confused.

My theory was confirmed two weeks later, when we got our exams back at the end of class. Lizzie quickly tucked her sheet into her school bag while Matt was looking over his own paper. I had caught sight of the 93% on the top right corner in Mr. Ray's red marker before she'd folded the paper, but as Matt turned back with his own sheet, a 74% in red ink circled at the top, hers was already out of sight.

"What'd you get?" he asked her.

"72%," she answered, smiling brightly. "Whew! I thought I was gonna do soooooo much worse than that."

"What about you, Kareema?" he asked, looking over at my paper, still open on top of my binder as I packed up my textbook. "95%," he said, and whistled. "Man, do you ever do anything but study? You gotta get out more."

"Don't be mean, Matt," Lizzie said, coming to my defense. "If it wasn't for her, we would both be lost in this class."

As we walked out of the lab, my face burned with anger and resentment. I had done Matt and Lizzie's in-class work for two months, taken all the notes, solved all the experiments in lab while they flirted together. He had spoken to me only to get the solutions he'd need to get passable grades, and I had given him the answers, and he still thought he could talk down to me and insult me!

Instead of turning at the washrooms with Lizzie as I usually did, I kept walking to the lockers, and as I walked, I realized I was mad at her too. We were supposed to be friends, and we had signed up for this course together, but for two months, she had almost completely ignored me all through class just so she could talk to a boy, so she could giggle as he insulted the teacher and pretend she thought he was funny. And for what? Didn't she already have a boyfriend? Didn't she like him?

Somehow, my anger that afternoon gave me the strength to decide I no longer cared to impress Matt. Sure, he was cute. In fact, for half a semester I was sure I really liked him; enough to pull my bangs out of the front of my *hijab*, enough to suck my stomach in all through fourth period until I could barely breathe, enough to avoid my mom's home cooking for fear I was getting fat, enough to miss the bus home every night while I wiped the make up off my face that I didn't want my mother to see, but at the end of the day, I didn't like him enough to play dumb for him. And that was that.

Then there was the question of Lizzie. As I rode the bus home, I thought about how to tell her I was mad at her, but where would I even start? The truth was, she hadn't done anything differently in Chemistry class than she had since high school had started, but this time I hadn't known anyone else in the class to hang out with and talk to instead. And what could I say to her that wouldn't be a total slap in the face? How could I say I thought she acted stupid for boys who weren't worth it? What kind of friend would I be then? In the end, I concluded that I couldn't have that conversation, and I kept the disappointment inside me, deciding instead that I just wouldn't be able to depend on her the way I thought I could, that I wouldn't sign up for anymore classes with her alone, or that at least, I wouldn't expect her to look out for me if I did.

As for the makeup, though I was no longer trying to impress Matt, I couldn't bring myself to just switch back. How could I, I reasoned, after eight weeks of red lipstick and covered up pimples, go back to nothing? I had to admit that even if I would never be the pretty girl, I did look better with my forehead clear of its acne, and with my eyes highlighted with a bit of eyeliner, I was a significantly prettier Kareema, a Kareema I wasn't sure I was quite ready to say goodbye to.

Despite my anger with her, I continued to meet Lizzie in the washroom before class for the next week, doing my makeup side by side with her, until one Monday morning, she didn't show up. In Social Studies, there was no sign of her, and neither Christianne nor Brenda had any idea where she was. At noon, when we arrived at our lockers to eat lunch, we found her standing there crying, her makeup a complete mess, tears awash with mascara streaming down her red cheeks, shoulders shaking.

"Oh my God, Lizzie," I called out, dropping my bag to the floor and running over to hug her. "What happened?"

Her whole body shook in my arms, and I could feel the wetness of her tears soaking into my shirt.

"We broke up," she finally moaned. "Jason and I broke up."

"Oh, Lizzie, I'm so sorry," I said. By now, Christianne and Brenda had crowded around us, and Brenda was stroking Lizzie's hair.

"Never mind him, Liz," Brenda said. "He's a jerk. He doesn't know what he's lost."

Lizzie's sobbing got harder, and Brenda led her away from us, down the hall to the washroom. Christianne and I stood dumbfounded, looking after them for a minute.

"Wow," I finally said. "I didn't see that coming."

"I kind of did," Christianne responded. "They got into a really big fight at the party on Saturday."

"There was a party on Saturday?" I asked. I was used to missing this kind of news. Everyone knew I didn't go to these parties, so no one really bothered inviting me anymore.

"Yeah. She was flirting with some guy in eleventh grade, and he was flirting with some girl in twelfth grade, and neither of them seemed to care, and then suddenly they were yelling at each other and …" her voice trailed off. "It wasn't pretty. I'm not really sure what she saw in him in the first place. Except maybe –" she glanced up at me, afraid to say what she was about to say, "except maybe that he's in twelfth grade and he played on the basketball team last term."

I nodded slowly. "Yeah. Actually, I don't think she's ever really gone out with very many nice guys."

"Nope," Christianne said, looking down at her feet, unable to continue this breach of all our high school rules eye to eye, "it doesn't really seem to be the main criteria."

And just like that, we were admitting everything we'd noticed about Lizzie since day one, admitting how every boyfriend she'd ever had seemed to break her heart, how it seemed more important to her to have a boyfriend than to be respected by the people she was around.

"So, what happened after the fight?" I finally asked.

"Oh, they acted like everything was all good. They drank, they danced, and they left at the end of the party still together. It wasn't the first time they fought about her flirting. Actually, I think she's gotten into a fight like that with every one of them."

It was that day, after that conversation that my feelings toward Lizzie shifted from jealousy to pity. Sure, she was the pretty girl, but she was also so many other things she didn't want to be, and at the same time missing so many things she could have been, as a result. It was true that everyone wanted to sit next to her, but once they sat, the goal had been achieved and they quickly ran out of things to say. Lizzie's life revolved around whom she was seen with, not what she was doing at the time, or whether she actually enjoyed doing it.

The rest of tenth grade passed in a blur, my days swimming into each other as I found everything had changed in the two classes I had made my entire focus. In Canadian Literature, I watched Christianne excel and enjoy herself doing something she truly loved, and while I myself was bored with the subject, I didn't want it to affect my average, and worked hard on my assignments while finally admitting to myself that I had signed up for the class for all the wrong reasons. In Chemistry, I continued to do the bulk of the work for Lizzie and Matt at our lab bench, but no longer did I pay much attention to their flirting. I slowly felt myself drifting from Lizzie as I focused more and more on the subject at hand and less on how to look a certain way while doing it. I made friends with another tenth grader in the class, a petite, shy girl named Felicity I had ignored on the first day of high school two years earlier precisely because she was exactly the kind of friend I used to have in junior high.

Through all of this, I continued to wear the makeup, although by now, I was putting it on each morning with Lizzie only because I was too afraid of what my classmates would say or think if I suddenly stopped wearing it.

Whereas in previous years, I was partially saddened by the coming of summer because it meant seeing less of my school friends, I welcomed it that year with open arms of relief. I needed time to myself, time away from the jungle of hallways and maze of criticism and judgment to decide who I really was. I remember waking up that first morning after the last day of school, washing my face in the washroom I shared with my younger brothers, and realizing I wouldn't be putting on any makeup. I stared a long time at my reflection, at my eyes, without the eyeliner underneath and mascara on top, my cheeks and my chin and forehead, the little pimples on them that wouldn't be hidden by any cover up for the rest of the summer, before turning off the lights and walking out of the washroom with a quiet resolve to join my family in the kitchen for breakfast.

Summer gave me some much needed perspective, helped me see life as more than just the time I spent in that miniature world of my school with my friends and classmates. My world revolved instead around my parents and my siblings, around the other Muslims I saw at study circles and Sisters' Soccer on Monday mornings at the near-by community centre. For the first time in what felt like ages, most of the girls around me didn't seem focused on hair, clothes, and makeup. They seemed more driven by other concerns: the older ones talked a lot about doing well in school. Many had to start applying for university that coming fall, and they stressed the importance of good grades for getting into the programs they wanted, and even getting scholarships.

"You're lucky, *masha Allah*," I remember one girl named Fatima telling me. "I want to apply for neuroscience, but I don't think I'll have the grades. Have you thought about what you want to take in university?"

I realized as she asked me that I hadn't. I had been so busy trying to survive the jungle of high school popularity that eventually it had become my entire life. I had pushed my family to one side and my personality to the other. I had done my schoolwork in shame that I could do it so well, and tried on identity after identity in vain, failing to become any of the things I had wanted so badly to be. After two years of failed identities, I was back where I'd started: still the smart girl. But for the first time, it occurred to me that maybe that wasn't such a bad thing to be. All this time, the prospect of university had seemed so foreign, so far away, but after all, wasn't the whole point of high school to learn, to do well enough that you would be ready for university?

As the school year approached, I packed the modest stash of makeup (three tubes of lipstick, one bottle of cover up and an eyeliner pencil) I had kept hidden in the top drawer of my dresser into a plastic bag and put it at the very bottom of my schoolbag, where no one would be able to find it. Christianne, Brenda, Lizzie and I had agreed to meet in the cafeteria on the first day before going to stake out a row of lockers we could claim, but I arrived early and made a detour to a washroom on the first floor, waiting until it was completely empty before pulling out my plastic bag and shoving it into the garbage, under a few wet paper towels. I was determined to start the year on a fresh page.

Once again, owing to the fact that we were taking Maths and Sciences, Lizzie and I had more classes together than we did with Christianne and Brenda. This time, it was grade 11 Math and Biology that we had, while all four of us would be going to English together. I had dreaded this realization as the summer wore on, feeling in my heart now that, unlike with Christianne and Brenda, I was more friends with Lizzie simply because we always had been, and not because we actually had anything in common. Our Biology class was second period, after English, and worried as I was that it would be a repeat of Chemistry the year before, my anxiety grew as we approached the classroom. How would I tell Lizzie I didn't want to be her lab partner? I wondered whether she even wanted to be mine, considering she would probably spend most of the term ignoring me to chat with whoever she was currently crushing on. In the end, the problem solved itself in the form of Derek, the guy who was on the verge of becoming Lizzie's next boyfriend, turning out to be in the same class.

"Oh my God," I remember her squealing as she grabbed my arm, "he's here! That's Derek, Kareema. I'm *totally* in love with him. He doesn't even know I'm alive though."

How shallow her words had suddenly sounded. Really, hadn't she been in love with Jason, and Matt, and Andrew? Outwardly, I feigned the proper 'good friend' excitement. "Of course he knows you're alive Liz. He's probably in love with you too. I think you'd look really cute together."

Meanwhile, I scanned the classroom desperately for another person I could partner up with. Please God, I thought, don't let this be another term of me doing all the work while my group ignores me. There had to be someone else I could work with, and there was: Felicity. I waved at her quickly as we took our temporary seats while the textbooks were handed out. I was ready to work with Felicity and whomever she picked, ready to be part of the nerd group if I had to be, in order to avoid my last year's fate. When the teacher announced that we would be split into groups of two, Lizzie looked at me apologetically as she explained that this was her only chance to talk to Derek. "Do you mind, Kareema?"

"No, it's okay," I answered, "I can work with someone else."

And so it was that Felicity and I were biology lab partners and got to know each other better over our worm and frog dissections, and over the sound of Lizzie's shrieking and giggling five benches away.

Along with Lizzie's outfit on the first day of school, I'll never forget a conversation Christianne and I had one noon hour in twelfth grade. We were alone at our lockers, Brenda being at the gym for basketball practice, while Lizzie was in the bleachers, alternatively cheering on both Brenda and a guy on the boys' senior team she never dated in the end.

We were three months from the end of high school, three months from the end of the world as we knew it, and we felt a certain fear, mixed with exhilaration, felt big in our possibilities when we looked at the future, and small as we noticed that we would be starting the equivalent of ninth grade all over again that next September. Some of us were getting ready to remake ourselves into the next incarnation, to shake off the identities that had followed us around for the last four years and wear a different cloak, or else to refine what we had become, to slowly move into that other realm which was the adult world.

I'm not sure at which point it dawned on me that I had decided I would just be myself, just be plain old Kareema, the smart girl, but also all the rest of me that I had been so unsure of four years earlier:

the Muslim girl, the girl who had black, unruly curls that you couldn't see because she wore *hijab*, and that was fine, the girl who liked skating with her younger brothers more than going to parties, who wasn't a size two, who was bad at tennis but okay at soccer, the girl who could write a good poem if the mood moved her, which wasn't often, but was still important, the girl who wanted to be a scientist. I think I realized this the morning earlier that week, when Lizzie had come to school with her hair dyed a platinum blonde and cut short on her head, wearing tighter jeans than usual with a rip across the knee and another one along the thighs.

Lizzie was preparing for a new identity, still the pretty girl, but this time pretty in that edgy, *don't mess with me* way, and I was sad for her, because I knew in my heart she would still feel messed with at the end.

We crowded around her as we always had, used to our roles, knowing the drill by now: "Oh my God!" one of us would say.

"You look Gorgeous!" another would continue. And on and on, with "I love its" and "it brings out your eyes" and every other compliment we had memorized in our four year runs as Lizzie's admirers, whether we meant it or not.

But now, Lizzie was in the bleachers at the gym and Christianne and I were sitting alone at our lockers, with the last four years behind us and the future so close and so far away that we suddenly felt the need to be honest. The question came out of my mouth before I knew it was even there, before I realized I needed to know if I was the only one who saw the act we'd been playing.

"Christianne?" I said.

She looked up from her notebook, the page half scribbled with a snippet of a poem she had to finish for her writing class that afternoon.

"Yeah?"

"Do you think Lizzie's pretty?"

Christianne paused a moment. "I think… I think she spends a lot of time making herself pretty. I think she... I think you're actually a lot prettier than she is."

I looked up at her surprised, took in her loose peasant shirt and worn out jeans, her simple ponytail.

"You know what? I think you're a lot prettier than her too" I told her, realizing I meant it and wasn't just returning a compliment, realizing my friend was actually a beautiful person, that I'd overlooked this all through high school since the pretty girl position had always been occupied and we had been silly enough to think there was only ever room for one of every type.

"It's just like she tries too hard sometimes." Christianne added.

I nodded, understanding completely. "That's exactly what it's like."

We went to different universities and colleges, Brenda leaving town on a sports scholarship, Christianne moving across the country for a specialized writing program that took four years to finish, and Lizzie and I at the two different universities in town. Oddly enough, though we were the only ones to stay in the city, Lizzie and I lost touch (despite promises otherwise in our final yearbooks) while I still speak often with Brenda and Christianne. Felicity, my lab partner in grade 11 Biology, was often my lab partner through out university; my lab partner, my study partner, and my friend.

This is My Fear

This is my fear
Of disconnecting from the connected world
Heart and mind exist as two
Not fused, not allied
But alone
Each in its own world of sentiments and logic
When to join forces would be much wiser
Yet wisdom creeps not into the atmosphere
Seeps not into the air
Wisdom is taught and sought
And sometimes fought
But I would not
That it be rejected
For wisdom is the lost property of the believer
And I am a believer

This is my fear
That fear itself guides me,
Paralyzes me, hides me
From the true path
That few walk down
But so many look up

This is my fear
My fear of no words
Of falling without words
Until they lose their meaning
Or I fail to comprehend them

This is my fear
Of the attribution of human mistakes
To divine systems
Those burned steer far away from all orange flames
And sometimes even orange balloons and cones
They miss more than they meant to avoid
Sometimes, much more
Sometimes they miss life

Picture Perfect—Kind Of

It was about the same time that I finally made the decision to wear *hijab*, that I knew I needed to share my new life as a *Muslimah* with my family. Up until then my sister and mother had known, but I hadn't found the courage to tell anyone else. Wearing *hijab* made things at once easier and more challenging. It made things more challenging in many ways. Most importantly, as I come from a secular Canadian family, wearing *hijab* made me feel naked in the sense that I was exposed to their judgment, something I wasn't sure I was strong enough to handle yet. But it also made things easier for me, because *hijab* speaks for itself somehow. Of course, it doesn't do the important job of explaining to concerned relatives what it means to be Muslim and to believe in Allah *subhaanahu wa t'ala*, but it does complete the difficult task of delivering shocking news. It was the initial statement that I so feared, in the months following my *shahada*. I couldn't figure out how to get the words out of my mouth: "Dad, I'm Muslim!" I wished he could guess and then ask me, "Are you Muslim?" because to answer, "Yes" would be much easier than to utter the entire statement. But wearing *hijab* meant that I could no longer avoid telling my father, my grandparents, my uncles and aunts. Wearing *hijab* meant that my faith was visible, and that I had no opportunity to hide anymore.

It was around then that the women of my mother's family decided it was time for a nice family photo–you know, with a photographer and coordinated outfits and everything. And so the planning began, and I was informed that the girls would be wearing white. The first thought to come to my mind of course was that I needed to find something appropriate to wear in white. I'm really not a fan of shopping, but I managed to find a *hijab* which I thought my mom might appreciate. It was white... maybe not meant to be a *hijab*, but it would work. It looked kind of like a table doily, only long and rectangular! Satisfied, I put the *hijab* away, and with it the thoughts of our photo shoot, and worries of my family's reaction. Since I became Muslim, Allah has blessed me with a more peaceful attitude towards stress and hardships. Although I was extremely nervous to see my family, and dreading it a little, I didn't let the thought of it consume me anymore. I put it aside to be dealt with in due time.

A couple of months later the family photo day arrived. We all congregated in Toronto at my aunt's house, since she has young twins –two year old bundles of energy. At first I was worried that my little cousins would be afraid of me with my *hijab*. "Maybe they'll think I look strange or scary," I thought to myself. But children are not born with prejudices, these are only taught as they grow older. They didn't even seem to notice anything different about me.

My aunt showed us to the basement where we would be sleeping –my mum, my sister and I. As we unpacked I told my mum about the white *hijab*, but she didn't seem as thrilled as I was. "Can't you show just a little bit of your hair?" she asked. I just smiled and said, "No mum, not really." When she told me she missed my hair I reminded her cheerfully that she could see it anytime, no problem! Mum has since become much more comfortable with everything, but of course these things take time.

I busied myself with other thoughts–mostly worrying about *salat*. This was before I was so blessed with the knowledge of shortening prayers during travel. I wondered how I would manage to sneak down there to pray four times throughout the day without making a scene. How would I wake up for *fajr* without freaking my mum out? The squeaky air-mattress and creaky wood floors were not working in my favour. I figured out the direction of the *Qibla* and evaluated potential prayer spaces.

When my grandparents arrived they were gracious and fully focused on the little ones. It is so refreshing to have children around in family gatherings. It becomes hard for tension to manifest when there are tiny footsteps and laughter and food being thrown around the room. We all take ourselves just a little less seriously when children are amongst us. *Masha Allah*, children truly are miracles in themselves.

Nobody really said anything at first about me being Muslim. It seemed they were all too afraid to mention it. Of course when my grandmother finally asked me about the scarf I had been wearing, and whether there was some sort of Muslim church I was attending, everyone who had wanted to ask questions but had been too polite hovered nearby and tried to busy themselves with drying dishes or washing up, while listening to our conversation. It was then that the questioning period began with my aunt, the lawyer. Ever since she started practicing law, our family has thrown around lawyer jokes. At the risk of sounding as though I mock her, I certainly appreciated her questions, but as she is very intelligent and thinks quickly, I did feel a little bit as though I were being cross examined!

When time for *salat* came, I did manage to duck out of the room and down to the basement quite discreetly. I found myself a little spot between the desk and the wall to pray, and it wasn't until half-way through the prayer that my very tall uncle wandered downstairs looking for something and didn't notice me behind the desk. He actually tripped over me while I was in *sajdah*, cornering himself between me praying, and the wall! It was all I could do to try desperately to focus on my prayer and not on his nervous apology or the fact that my face was turning a bright tomato-red. When I went back into *sajdah* he took the opportunity to leap over me and then scrambled back upstairs. I'm not sure which one of us felt most embarrassed.

My *salat* adventures aside, things went altogether quite smoothly. When the time for the actual photos arrived, we trundled out to a little patch of forest where the photographer positioned us amidst branches and rocks, in different combinations based on height, age, family tree, and so on. It is an odd feeling to stand in front of a camera with your family and feel that you stick out so much, but it was a good experience to go through. I think the only reason looking different bothers me, is that it is reflective of a much more significant difference within; a difference in belief. Feeling so apart from my family in such a fundamental way has been a great test for me in my faith. I suppose it is something that takes a long time to adapt to, and everything gets easier with time. Who knows what the future holds as well, the best I can do is remain hopeful.

There was one small moment at dinner that night which I found quite touching. You see, my sister has also recently developed faith in God. She has been attending a Baptist church for a few months now, with her boyfriend's family. In a sense this brought a bit of relief to the situation, as most of the family seems to find it quite hilarious that such secular parents could raise a Baptist and a Muslim. So as we sat around the dinner table my grandmother surprised me when she asked my sister if she would like to say grace for us. I couldn't remember the last time we had said grace together, or even if we ever had.

My sister is younger than me, and is obviously going through her own struggle in dealing with everyone's reactions to a sudden development of faith, but she handled it with her usual charisma. Much to my amusement my aunt then spoke up, and asked me if there was something else I would like to say before eating? I appreciated the efforts of my family in trying to make things less awkward for us. Also feeling put on the spot, I laughed a little and told them I would basically say the same as my sister, just without the 'in Jesus' name' part at the end! Then I mentioned the use of *Bismillah* before starting anything, especially a meal. At the sound of Arabic my grandfather searched his memory for any words stored there from his army service in Egypt long ago. "*Yalla!*" was about all he could remember, which I thought sounded very cute from him.

And so went the first meeting with my family as an openly practicing Muslim. It is always good to get firsts over with, because the more they loom ahead of us the more our imaginations create all the worst scenarios. Being a procrastinator in these situations, as with anything, only makes things easier temporarily. But the time to deal with them comes one day or the next. I'm sure the future will be full of awkward moments and misunderstandings between my family and I, but there is also a great amount of humour in this, which I find I can appreciate now. It seems the most important thing is to have conviction, and to be comfortable with yourself so that you may set the tone for everyone else as well.

I pray for guidance in dealing with my family, that I may always be kind and understanding with them.

Unshakable Truths

Unshakable truths that just don't hold up
They may not shake, but they crumble
The arrogance of the human mind
That believes it has reached absolute truth from its own doings
Life experiences are general and specific at the same time
But they are yours, not mine
Because if we let only our experiences guide us
We would be completely misguided
Lost in the jungle of life and death
Hurting from the learning of one painful lesson and the next
There must be a simpler way
And there is
But humans gravitate towards complexity
Complicating matters, complicating life
Simplicity is beautiful, but beauty is in the eye of the beholder
Who beholds you?
Too many people to count
So don't count the people
Simplicity-One God
One Beholder
Life is simple
Humans are complex

Confessions of a Fallen Daughter

I've never enjoyed biology. In grade 9, I lost my silver earring during fourth period while dissecting a rat with my lab partner. We later found that earring lodged in our poor rat's small intestine. From then on, I never could seem to get myself fully immersed in that subject. Then in grade 10, the new sweater I had saved up for for months got splattered with bright red dye from our molecular probes experiment. The sweater was only two days old, and I was furious. Needless to say, the store refused my attempt at a refund. But, it was over the next few years that biology would throw me its hardest punch. I learned something about human physiology that no classroom could ever teach me: I discovered that the human brain could be a very stubborn organ and the tongue could sometimes be a foolish muscle indeed. The events I'm about to relay may seem insignificant or trivial to some, but let me assure you that while I was going through them they were anything but. You see, to be in a state of displeasing my parents hurts me more than anything in this world. And yet I don't do nearly enough to please them.

I have always thought of myself as the bad child of the family. As a child of 2 years old I would mimic my mother's reproaches diligently whenever she reprimanded me for something wrong I had done. Ever since then, I think I have been secretly trying to fill that role, and in all honesty, it's a role that no one assigned to me but myself. I don't write this to preach to you about respecting your parents, because Lord knows I'm the last person qualified to do that. I write this to free my guilt, rid my mind and heart of the pain of a fallen daughter, in the hopes that it may change me. I think my problem is that I can't seem to swallow my foolish pride. And when I do manage to take a gulp, I just can't seem to keep it down quite long enough. So what does it mean to be a fallen daughter, you ask?

It means tears welling up in your eyes for no reason at all, and for every reason big and small. It means guilt and shame bubbling inside of you. It is not the love of a fallen daughter that is doubted, it is her wisdom that is questionable. But enough with the theoretical babble, let's get to the heart of the matter: how I came to be fallen.

I believe it was a series of "embarrassing events" that first triggered me to begin falling. I had somehow come to the conclusion, after feeling mortified by my parents' actions on a few successive occasions, that it was okay to disrespect them.

It began with parent-teacher interviews in grade 10. I remember wishing the Earth would just open up and swallow me whole when my mother emerged from her bedroom dressed in our traditional Moroccan costume. She'd told me earlier that she wanted to look nice for the interviews and make a good impression on the teachers. *It's not like we're going to a wedding*, I thought to myself, *or a circus for that matter*. But I bit my tongue and tried my best to lag a few steps behind her on the off chance that I might get lucky and people might not assume that we were together. Of course, that plan fell through when my mother insisted on linking arms with me so we wouldn't lose each other as we traversed the crowded halls, from classroom to classroom.

We made our rounds and my mother happily met all my teachers, chit-chatting with them in her broken English. I tried to rush her through each meet and greet; she took her sweet time. To my great horror, it wasn't just my teachers that my mother enthusiastically chatted with, she also went out of her way to meet my friends. "Oh and zis is za Jillian/Amanda/Mandy I hear all the time about?" she would chirp, "Iz lovely to meet you". In this way, she introduced herself to all my friends. And my friends, out of their common courtesy, pretended to be interested and played along. Or at least that's what I assumed their chit-chat was. By the end of the night, there was just no hiding it: the woman sporting the multicoloured headscarf and long, bright cloak of sorts who spoke English with a thick Arabic accent was my mother. Everybody knew it; some, at least, tried to hide their pity for me, when, to be honest, I was having a hard time hiding my pity for myself.

At the very end of the night, just when I thought it couldn't get any worse, my chemistry teacher, Mrs. Jamieson, called out to my mother as we were gathering our things. "Mrs. Bendjoud, thank you for coming this evening, it was nice to have met you."

"I'm nicer," my mother replied, taking Mrs. Jamieson's hands in hers and shaking vigorously, "I'm nicer really, I'm nicer," my mother muttered again.

I'm nicer!? What in the world!? How embarrassed was I? My mother was obviously trying to translate an Arabic expression that is often said when two people depart after meeting. It can be roughly translated as: "I'm happy I had the opportunity to meet you" whereupon the other person replies: "I'm happier". But apparently my mother didn't realize that happy and nice were not synonyms, so as Mrs. Jamieson tried to hide the confusion on her face, I tried to hide the utter embarrassment on mine.

For some reason, it was those kinds of incidents that stood out in my mind, leaving me with the perpetual fear that my mother would "embarrass" me in front of anyone and everyone that mattered, or didn't matter for that matter. My confirmation bias worked such that I conveniently overlooked all the love, joy and sacrifice my mother showered me with, only to remember the times she mispronounced a word or dressed in her colourful style. It was around that time that I reached the gross assumption that my mother's opinions and advice didn't matter. I began to reject everything she tried to give me. After all, I told myself, I was raised here so I know more about what's appropriate in this culture than she does. And though I did know the language, expressions and American culture better than anyone else in my family, very few could outmatch my mother's wisdom and knowledge of the ways of the world. Very few could inspire so much with the gentlest of nudges. Very few could comfort so deeply with the slightest touch. But only with time did I see this. Only with time did I realize how insignificant it was to know that "da bomb" and "wicked" were actually good things. Only with time did I see that, though the icing on top may have been missing, I had all the good things one could ever want in life. But my own eyes were blind to these blessings. I looked at them everyday but did not see them. Since they had always been a part of my life, I assumed they were a part of everyone else's life too. It was Lillith who, in part, made me see that that was not the case. Through her fresh pair of eyes, I began to see, for the first time, what I had often overlooked. Looking back now, I think there's something very sad about that.

When I was in grade twelve, I convinced my parents to allow me to sign our family up as a host family to an international student on exchange. Lillith Burnaby-Green, from Liverpool England, lived with us for an entire semester. She arrived on September 1st, a few days before school started, and settled into our family routine nicely. Lillith was a thoughtful, wise young woman who maintained an open-minded approach to life. I didn't find this out until later, but Lillith had asked to be placed with an Arab family if possible, a request I couldn't possibly fathom at the time. When Lillith arrived, I was delighted. In my mind, I saw her as my ticket to fitting in and distancing myself from my parents. We would go to and from school together everyday, though we didn't share all the same classes. It was my hope that Lillith's presence could undo some of what my parents' presence had done. When people saw me with her everyday, I prayed, they would associate me with the white girl instead of the immigrant parents. But Lillith, it turned out, had her own plan. She arrived ready and eager for change. She wanted to learn as much as possible about our way of life and found my mother to be a very good and kind teacher. My mother enjoyed sharing everything we did with Lillith, our cuisine, our customs. She would often pray her five daily prayers in front of Lillith, and even ask her before beginning prayer if there was anything in particular she would like her to pray for. I, on the other hand, kept with my five daily prayers, but kept with them in secret. If Lillith was around when it was time for prayer, I would slip out of the room discretely and duck into my parents' room, closing the door behind me so Lillith could not see what I was doing. But Lillith was persistent and perceptive. One time, Lillith even asked my mother if she could join her in prayer. She beamed as my mother helped her wrap one of her colourful headscarves around her head. Then she stood respectfully next to my mother and followed my mother's every move, bowing and prostrating while watching my mother's body out of the corner of her eye.

I think Lillith could sense that I wasn't entirely comfortable talking about our differences. She never asked me why I didn't pray in front of her when the rest of my family lined up for prayer. My mother would announce that they were going to pray and I would respond that I already had and that would be that. But Lillith couldn't help asking about the little things, even with me:

"What is it that you say after you make plans?" she asked me one day, after I had just hung up the phone with my cousin, arranging to meet her at a volleyball game that Saturday. I looked over at her attentively.

"You know," she prompted, "something like ansha…shalla, you all say it all the time."

"Oh," I piped up, "you mean *insha Allah*?"

"That's it!" she said, trying it out a few times to herself. "*Inshallah*," she said aloud in her British accent. "What does it mean?"

"It means God willing," I replied

"Hmmm…I like that…*inshallah*. Because you never know what fate will bring," she said smiling.

"Yeah, I guess," I replied. I had never really given it much thought until that day, to be honest. It was something I had just learned to slip into my speech, probably because my parents said it all the time. The difference, though, is that they probably meant it when they said it, while for me, it was just a passing expression. But it did make sense to me when I thought about it. And from that day on, I made a point to say it more often when I was around Lillith, in an attempt to impress her. I don't know why I felt I needed her approval before I could practice my way of life.

At school, my plan was working. The majority of our class was intrigued by Lillith and her charming British accent. The appeal was probably heightened because our town didn't get many visitors. "What do you call pants?" they would ask. "What about garbage?" "Trousers and rubbish," Lillith would reply as students listened in fascination, asking if she'd ever seen Prince William or the Queen. Though Lillith didn't talk about her family much, I had them all figured out in my head. She had showed us a family photo once, with herself, her older brother and her younger sister sitting on the porch steps while her mom and dad stood behind them, smiling in the summer breeze. Jealousy bubbled inside of me every time I thought of that photo. Why couldn't I have had that perfect family and a normal soccer mom like everyone else? I was completely clueless to the fact that Lillith would exchange families with me in a heartbeat, and that she would definitely be getting the better end of the deal if she did. I had no idea that one of the driving forces that had led Lillith right here to my home was to be as far away from her family as possible.

One night, after Lillith had been with us for a month and a half, she whispered something to me in the darkness, her soft voice filling the quiet room.

"Ever since I arrived, I knew there was something special about this home," she said, not knowing if I was asleep or awake. I was dosing off at that point, but her words quickly woke me up.

"Really?" I asked. I was genuinely surprised by her comment. My home…special?

"Yes, really. For the longest time I couldn't put my finger on it. I couldn't figure out what made this home so serene. But I think I finally figured it out," she mused.

"Soooooooo," I said, "tell me what it is, the suspense is killing me," I joked.

But Lillith's tone was serious and solemn.

"There's no yelling in your house." She paused for a moment, "And no alcohol to make people yell," she said.

We both lay there quietly for a few minutes, staring off into the darkness of the night, listening to the sound of our breath as it rose and fell. I felt like I should say something to Lillith, comfort her, help her cope with the hurt in her life. But I didn't want to pry into her personal life. Besides, her family looked so perfect, what could possibly be the matter, I thought? So I just lay there quietly, staring at the ceiling and breathing deeply.

"You're very blessed you know," she finally said. "But somehow, I don't think you do know," she said in a slightly lowered voice. "Good night Sara." And with that, Lillith turned on her side and buried her head in her pillow. I shut my eyes and pretended to fall asleep. But the words Lillith had spoken echoed in my mind. What had she meant, I wondered?

But despite Lillith's immense appreciation for my wonderful parents, something happened that rekindled my shame of them. And not too long after she was on a plane back to England, I was cooking up a way to distance myself from them again. It was right after graduation that my fallenness hit an all time low. Instead of random acts of kindness, I began to execute random acts of disrespect toward my parents. In my heart, however, I felt I was justified because my parents had ruined my graduation.

All my life, I had pictured in my mind exactly how that day would be. And then my parents walked in and shattered that picture. Graduation was supposed to be perfect. But it turned out to be anything but, and all because of my parents. Leading up to the big day, everything was just hunky dory. I had eaten a good hearty breakfast (compliments of my mom), I had met up with all my friends backstage, and I had been given a cap and gown that fit me well, unlike some less fortunate students that stumbled around in theirs. As my friends and I lined up in our places, getting ready for the commencement ceremony, there was a surge of excitement in the room. My big moment was coming, I thought. This is it, my fifteen minutes of fame. The distinct sound of the bagpipes summoned us out into the auditorium and we marched earnestly, proudly, excitedly, waving at friends and family, until we took our seats in silence. I myself didn't do any waving. No need to draw unnecessary attention to my family. Nothing could take this feeling from me now, I thought to myself as I stared at the high school diplomas and awards lining the auditorium's stage. But there was one thing that could do it—my parents of course. For if my parents faltered but slightly, I always blew a gasket.

I watched my classmates stride up onto the stage, one by one, accepting their diplomas and happily staring back at the flickering camera flashes. Soon it would be my turn, I thought. And then it was. "Sara Bendjoud" the principal called. The crowd erupted in applause. I glided across the stage merrily. And then, I saw it. I couldn't believe it; it was like a nightmare I couldn't rouse myself from. My mother and father, both of them, were standing right under me, in front of the stage, trying to position themselves to be in my picture as I walked across the stage. Ali, my brother, standing further back, tried to take the picture. But as my mother scurried to get in the shot, she tripped on her skirt and toppled over onto the auditorium floor, in front of all 600 guests. My father, in his attempt to break my mother's fall, grabbed her right hand, only to end up tumbling down beside her. This time, the auditorium erupted in laughter instead of applause. And I turned into one giant tomato right up there on the stage in front of everyone.

Needless to say, I didn't take this little mishap by my parents at all well. While others rushed out of their seats to make sure my parents were both okay, I rushed off the stage and felt like rushing into a cave where I would hide for the rest of my life. My brother found the whole incident hysterical and tried to joke with me about it, telling me to "lighten up, it was just an accident". But I could not see it as anything other than a sign that I needed to escape my wacky parents. The rest of that day was quite something, with my parents and Ali laughing off the whole thing and resuming life as normal, while I made a strong effort to display just how perpetually embarrassed I was at every possible moment. After the reception in our school's cafeteria, which I mainly spent dodging my parents, my father suggested that he take us out for lunch at my favourite restaurant. "No, that's okay," I replied "I'd rather go home and sleep". I was bent on remaining in a grouchy mood and prolonging my misery. I started my summer off in a sour mood and ended it off in the exact same way. Bitterness festered inside of me, bitterness that later lead me to do things of which I am not at all proud.

Exhibit A:

It was summer and I was relatively free. I had gotten a part-time summer job at the local community centre, planning summer activities, but other than that, I had time on my hands. My mother knocked on my door early one morning. I think it was about 8:30 am. "Sara *habibty*?" she whispered. "Sara, could you please wake up?" She spoke in Arabic of course, and I pulled the covers up over my head and turned the other way. "Sara, I'm not feeling very well," she continued, "I'm going to go see a doctor, do you think you could please come with me?"

"I have plans," I muttered from under my covers. "Take Ali with you."

My mother stood in the doorway for a moment, before I heard my bedroom door close again. About ten minutes later I heard the car pull out of the driveway. I got out of bed at noon that day. My plans were to sleep in and meet my friends for brunch after, obviously something that couldn't be missed to accompany my ill mother to the doctor's office.

Exhibit B:

It was August and summer was drawing to an end. My friends and I were all preparing for the upcoming school year. My friend Adrianna was throwing a goodbye party at her house for all our friends who would be going off to University out of town in the fall. It would be an all girls bash and we decided we would all dress up super soirée style. For an entire month before the party, I was hunting for that perfect dress. And then one day, tucked away deep in the back of the department store, I came upon it. It was a blue and white evening gown, with thick velvet straps and a long flowing style—it was gorgeous. Not only that—it was on sale. I smiled broadly to myself, unable to contain my excitement. I got out my cell phone and imme-diately called my mom. She picked up on the 5th ring.

"Mom," I exclaimed, "I found it I found it I found it!"

"Slow down there honey, what is it that you found?" We spoke in Arabic.

"The perfect dress...please...you have to come see it...please mom, could you come now...I'm at Sears. It's on sale and it's the last one. Do you think you could come now? Pleeeeeease!" I was aware of the fact that I sounded like a four year old, but I was that excited.

"Oh honey, I have that lunch with the Ladies at Auntie Hind's house in half an hour and you know how far she lives. We've been planning this for ages. It's the only time we could find to catch up and visit each other. Why don't you and I go to Sears together tomorrow and you can try it on for me then?"

"Tomorrow?" I whined "It could be gone by tomorrow...it's the last one and it's perfect. I already asked the cashier and she said it's final sale." I paused for a moment for dramatic effect. "Please Mama, it would mean so much to me."

I could hear my mother's soft sigh on the other end.

"Okay *habibty*, I'll have to call Auntie Hind to apologize and then I'll be right over."

"Oh thank you thank you thank you!" I gushed. I couldn't wait to try it on and see how it fit. My mother dropped everything and came that day even though I know she was really looking forward to visiting with all her friends again. She came to me wearing a fancy *abaya* and a nice smile. And I felt justified for having ruined my mother's plans when the dress fit absolutely perfectly. She paid for it and we headed home, I in an excited frenzy and she in a thoughtful mood. As we stepped into the house, she headed for the phone.

"I might still be able to catch them," she said. "You know how it is, we women like to go on and on." She picked up the phone and dialed Aunt Hind's telephone number. I only caught the last little bit of her conversation: "Okay then…maybe some other time *insha Allah*…you take good care…okay….*assalamu alaikum*."

My mother hung up the phone. "They've all already gone home." she said "That's okay, some other time *insha Allah*. Why don't you get that dress hung up so it doesn't need ironing before Friday?" she grinned. I flew up the stairs, dress in hand, unable to wipe the silly smile of glee off my face.

That Friday, my mother drove me to Adrianna's house for the party. As we approached the brightly lit house, my mother took my hand in hers and squeezed it.

"Have a great time *habibty*," she said. "I'll pick you up at 11:00."

Then she seemed to have suddenly remembered something.

"Didn't Adrianna's mother recently have her appendix removed?" she asked.

"Yeah," I replied, "but she got out of the hospital over a month ago."

"Still," my mother continued, "I should at least go in and say hi.

Visiting the sick is very important you know."

"No, please," I yelped. As I spoke these words, I was aware that they sounded very bad.

My mother looked at me, surprised.

"What's the problem honey? The woman was sick and I want to check on her. This is my duty. You're not ashamed of your own mother are you?"

The question hung there heavily, it lingered in the air like a foul smell. The truth was that I was ashamed of my own mother, and for very shallow reasons at that.

"Honey?" My mom repeated. I still hadn't answered her question.

After the most awkward silence in the world I finally spoke up, "It's just that…" I began, "It's just that you're not like the other moms. Please, could you just visit Mrs. Connaway some other time when all my friends aren't around?" With that I picked up my purse and opened the car door. My high heels hit the pavement and I heaved myself out of the car.

To this day, I still don't know how deeply that comment hurt my mother, but as I walked up the porch steps to the front entrance, I heard the car speed away. I didn't look back. It was Ali who came to pick me up at 11:00 that night.

I wish I could say that that incident was the only one of its kind, but unfortunately I can't. There are many more that I do not relay here, for some are just too painful to write out on paper. And maybe somewhere in the back of my mind, I believe that if I never speak of them again, they will magically disappear and I will conveniently forget. But I cannot forget. Believe me; I have been desperately trying for the past 4 years. When you wound someone, particularly someone who would give anything to see you happy, you cannot forget. In fact, you remember all too well.

The summer after the spectacle at my graduation, I conjured up elaborate plans for how to flee the curse of my parents. I would not let my parents destroy my future, I told myself. I would no longer allow others to judge me by my parents' eccentric actions. For how long would I allow myself to be plagued by their cultural nuisances? For how long would I walk in their shadows? I convinced myself that something urgently had to be done. But my elaborate escape plans would be of no use. I needed something realistic, something believable. And so I set out to persuade my parents that it was in my best interest to move out of our house and into the university residence at the start of the academic year. I had already been accepted to the university in our town, which was a good university, with a good reputation. But since we only lived about an hour's commute away, my parents had assumed that my choosing to study at our home-town university meant my continuing to live with the family. Not so, I would explain. It really would help me focus better on my studies if I was in the university environment. I could run off to the library whenever needed; I could drop in to talk to professors for clarifications on lectures. And I was guaranteed to be on time to all my classes, even if there was a terrible snow storm or a trans-portation strike. It was imperative, I would insist; it would greatly enhance my chances of high academic success.

We spent many long summer evenings discussing this, my parents and I. They would glance at each other from across the kitchen table as I sat there presenting my case, putting forth one argument after another. Though my family lived comfortably, we were not wealthy by any means and didn't have that kind of extra money to spare. But I chose to ignore that fact, they would find a way. And to my surprise, they did. My parents called me into their bedroom one evening, just after I had finished brushing my teeth.

"Sara *habibty*, could you please come in here a moment?" I heard them say. I stepped into their room, my mouth feeling minty fresh, and stood by their bed, where they were both sitting, the night lamp on their bedside table casting a shadow across their faces. They were both smiling.   I found myself inadvertently smiling too. Something was up, I thought.

"Sara, we've been thinking," my father began in Arabic, his shadow dancing on the wall as he spoke.

"We think we've found a way to make it possible for you to live in the university residence," my mom continued.

"We went over our budget and expenditures," my father explained, "and we found that if we cut something out, we could put that money toward the rent of the dorm room. So, instead of going to visit Morocco every two years, we'll just go every three years instead and use those savings."

"We've already spoken to Ali and he said he wouldn't mind," my mom reassured me. As they said this, an even larger smile broke across their faces. Parents always delight in being able to give their children what they want, even if it comes at a sacrifice to them. I felt a twang of guilt shoot through my body. Here I was about to accept a big gift from the two people I'd spent the past few months disrespecting and deceiving. Had I no shame at all? If I did, it must have been buried very deep inside of me that day, because all I could do was say, "Oh that's great, I'm so glad we could find a way to make this work, because it really will positively affect my studies insha Allah." No "thank you thank you thank you!", no "sorry for the way I've treated you recently (and not so recently)", and no hugs and kisses.

"So," my father continued, "if this is what you really want, we can all go take a look at the dorms tomorrow insha Allah."

"And I'll help you get started on the packing," my mother said.

"Oh and honey, remember to pray *salat al istikhara* before you make your final decision". We kissed each other good night and I headed off to my room where I spent the next 5 minutes jumping for joy. In my wild excitement, I completely forgot about something called *salat al istikhara*. This was it, the beginning of my new life. My chance to build a name for myself that would not be stained by my parents. This was my chance at independence, and I was absolutely thrilled.

By September, I was nicely settled into my new dorm room at the university with my new roommate Chantal. My parents and Ali had helped me pack my belongings and move them into the tiny room Chantal and I would be sharing. From our trips back and forth when I was first settling in, I noted that the drive between our house and my new place took about half an hour to 45 minutes depending on traffic, meaning the two places weren't exactly close by—definitely one of the highlights of this new arrangement.

At first, I reveled in my new found freedom, waking up at ridiculous hours of the afternoon and going to sleep at ridiculous hours of the night. I ate what I wanted when I wanted, often starting with dessert before moving on to…well…more junk food. I was on time to *almost* all my classes. It seems that the closer you live to your class, the more you rush to get there on time. My mother called me about twice a day at the beginning, checking up on me and making sure I had enough food. I always insisted that everything was just fine, even if the fridge was completely empty and my clothes were almost all dirty. I would get to it, I told myself, but somehow I never did. My roommate Chantal and I got along okay. I wouldn't exactly say we clicked, but we didn't argue constantly either, which was good for two complete strangers who shared such a small living space together. And even though we weren't quite buddies, I appreciated the fact that there was, at the very least, another breathing human being around. The intermittent fights we did have helped to distract me from my loneliness and homesickness.

It wasn't long before the allure of freedom wore off and the stress of freedom kicked in. By the second month of my first semester, I was in way over my head. I was dragging my feet to all my classes and yawning my way through my midterm exams. I had stopped answering most of my mother's phone calls, but was always secretly relieved to see her and my Dad when they came to pick me up on Friday afternoons to take me home for the weekend. My mother would come prepared with a big garbage bag which she would subsequently proceed to fill with all my dirty laundry, even as I insisted that I was "just about to get to it" and that I had everything under control. There came a point though when I was just too exhausted to care "how embarrassing" it would look and eagerly helped her pack all my dirty clothes in there. On Sunday evenings, before they would drive me back to my dorm, my mom would pack up an assortment of home cooked food for me in plastic containers. I always went on and on about how she didn't have to bother and how I could cook my own food now. Ignoring my jabber, my mother packed the food anyway, saying it would make her feel better if I just please took it. I always thanked God that she was more persistent than me.

Adjusting to university life was no small feat. The large class sizes, the impersonal treatment, the immense work load and the lack of follow-up all took me months to get used to. But that wasn't the hardest part. The hardest part was actually adjusting to my new living arrangements, the living arrangements I had fought so long and hard for, the living arrangements I had made my family sacrifice for. It was actually the little things that had the biggest effect on me; the things I never even realized existed until they weren't there anymore. Not waking up to my mother's soft voice in the morning or finding breakfast waiting for me at the breakfast table as I rushed off to school. Now all I found waiting for me in our tiny kitchenette as I bolted out to class were Chantal's dirty dishes from her late dinner the night before. I often found myself skipping breakfast entirely to make it to class on time, only to be reminded that my body needed food by the throbbing headache I would develop around noon. I also found myself missing the casual conversations I would have throughout the day with different family members. Whether it was my mother, my father or Ali, at home, there was always someone to talk to. Chantal worked two jobs to pay for her education and wasn't around much. When she was around, most of our conversations began with the words: "Have you seen my..." and could end with any number of words (i.e.: textbook, book report, assignment, sweater, watch, glasses etc.). At first, she'd go visit one of her parents once a month. Her parents were divorced and lived in two different cities, so she could only afford to buy a bus ticket to one of their places once a month. But that routine didn't last long. In November, she came back from one of her trips to her mom's house in tears and threw her luggage down on her bed, kicking her dresser as she passed it.

"Why do I even bother!" she yelled. "Why do I even bother making a five hour trip only to arrive and find that mommy dearest is too busy for her own daughter?!" She was too upset that night to get anything coherent out of her. But over the next few days she spilled it all. Apparently, when she had arrived at her mother's place she had found her mother, who was supposed to be expecting her, out on a date. She'd had to wait outside on the porch steps until 11:00 pm when her mother and her date finally got home to let her in. The next day, Chantal was told to order dinner in since her mother had another date. She'd made a five hour trip only to spend the evening alone sitting on her mother's couch, eating Chinese fried rice out of a box and flipping channels on the remote control. She tried to wait up for her mom, but fell asleep on the couch before her mom got back. So from then on, she stopped going to visit her parents except on holidays.She would spend Thanksgiving with her father and Christmas with her mother. And other than that, she would call the 'student cell' we shared home. "What a miserable existence," she would often say as she sat cramped in one of the four corners of our room. "No one should have to live in a shoebox for eight months out of the year."

Though I eventually got used to my new lifestyle, I never quite did get comfortable with it. But I worked very hard to make sure my parents wouldn't detect this. After all, I had built up this reputation as Miss Independent and didn't want my image to be tarnished. So as I bled on the inside, I glittered on the outside. My loneliness was outmatched only by my pride, so I went on pretending, pretending that my independence really was paving a better road for me in life. When in reality, all it was doing was digging me a deep hole.

Despite everything, I somehow survived my first year of university. When summer finally rolled around, I quietly thanked the Lord. It was back to healthy breakfasts and the background noise of human voices. It was back to waking up to the sound of laughter and singing. It was back to conversations that were longer than three words. It was back to living in a space that was larger than a walk-in closet. It was back to my parents, and for the first time in a long time, the thought of that didn't bother me.

Before Lillith had stepped on her plane back to England, we had agreed to keep in touch. And oddly enough, we actually had. We emailed each other regularly and kept each other posted on the current events of our lives. I told her all about how excited I was to start university and move into residence. She wrote to me about her volunteer work at the sick kid's hospital in Liverpool. Week in and week out Lillith and I exchanged updates and I think she eventually noticed my declining enthusiasm for my new living arrangements. Lillith may have been the only person I ever admitted to that I was feeling homesick and lonely when I was away from home. *I don't blame you*, she had written to me once, after I had finally opened up to her about my true feelings regarding my accommodations. *If I had a family like yours, I'd probably feel homesick even when I was   on vacation in Hawaii.*

In March, Lillith wrote to me asking if I was planning on taking any summer courses. Noooooooooooooooooooo, I replied; I was in dire need of a break. *Well then I have just the break for you*, she had

written. *Why don't you come visit me and my family in Liverpool?*
When I told my parents about the idea, their trust in me surprised
even me. "University has changed you you know," they had said. And
I couldn't have agreed more. University had opened my eyes. Nobody
in university cared if you showed up to class wearing your pajamas.
Nobody cared if you showed up to class period. We were all just
trying to survive in this big old world, trying to reach a destination,
accomplish a goal. And every person had a different way of accom-
plishing that goal. Some students brought their kids with them to
class because they couldn't find a last minute replacement for their
babysitter. Some students dropped out of class because they couldn't
keep up with the workload or afford to pay the course fees on time.
Every person had a different set of circumstances. Supportive parents
at the university level, I soon began to see, is a privilege not a right.
There really is great value in education, and it's not always contained
in your textbooks and lecture notes.

I still had some money saved up from my previous summer
jobs and could use that to pay for the plane ticket to England. Lillith
emailed me regularly to help finalize all the trip details and to remind
me that it would be her family's pleasure to host me during my
visit. My Dad helped me find and book a good deal online. My
mom helped me pack, making sure to include lots of little gifts for
the Burnaby-Green's, and the whole family drove me to the airport.
And then, I was off to England. I was off to experience life for ten days
with the model family that I had dreamt of all my life. This will
be a life changing experience, I told myself. And as it turned out, I
was quite right about that, but just not in the way I expected.

It was Lillith and her father that came to pick me up from
the airport. As I stepped out of the arrivals gate, bubbling with excitement, Lillith ran to greet me, hugging me and kissing me on the cheek
in the traditional Moroccan way just like my mother had taught her.
Her father stood off to the side, waiting for us to finish our shrieks of

joy before approaching to say hello. We walked over to the baggage claims area and waited to spot my suitcase, all the meanwhile Lillith and I jabbering away about who missed who more.

"And how are Adrianna and Daphne?" Lillith asked "Do you still see them?"

"Actually, they both moved to Boston for College. I haven't seen them since last summer. But Adrianna threw an awesome goodbye party for all the gals before she left. It was really great. I wish you could have been there."

"Me too," Lillith replied.

We settled into the car and began the drive back to their home, where I couldn't wait to meet the rest of the perfect family. It was about a 30 minute drive from the airport to their white single family home and Lillith and I spent the entire 30 minutes catching up with each other. When we arrived, Lillith's mother opened the front door for us, welcoming me with a smile and a hand shake and barking at her husband to move my suitcase to the upstairs hallway for now. After washing up and sitting down for dinner, Lillith's younger sister, Judith, emerged from upstairs and joined us at the dinner table, greeting me and introducing herself by saying: "Oh just call me Jay."

"It's jolly nice to finally meet you," she said. "You know, after Lillith came back from your place, she just wouldn't shut up about you and your family. They sound really brill."

I smiled back. "Oh, well, thank you." I think.

We ate dinner mostly in silence. I tried to think of something to say to break the ice, but I was just too nervous. I wanted more than ever to leave a good impression with these people and that was hindering my thought process.

Jay broke the silence after stuffing a forkful of roasted potatoes in her mouth: "So, you were smart enough to come for a visit when Randy was out of town," she began. "Randy is our bothersome older brother, just in case you don't know. Everyone agrees he should have been put up for adoption," she finished.

"Oh don't be a bloody idiot!" her father snapped, "You're the one we should have put up for adoption."

"John," her mom hissed, "please, we've got company."

Lillith fidgeted uncomfortably with her utensils, accidentally clanking them noisily on her plate.

"If I had wanted to hear a symphony over dinner, I would have played my Mozart record thank you very much," her father bellowed.

Lillith put her fork and spoon down on her plate beside the heap of potatoes she hadn't yet touched and turned to me: "If you're all done Sara, I can take you upstairs to our room so you can unpack your things," she said.

"Oh, sure," I answered. I put down my fork and pushed back my chair. "Thank you very much for dinner."

Lillith and I headed upstairs. Her bedroom was the first door on the left. She closed the door behind us and stood with her back against it.

"I'm sorry about that," she sighed deeply.

"Oh, no, don't worry about it." I pretended not to know what she meant, not to have noticed the general tension and awkwardness over dinner.

"They're usually able to put on an act for at least a few hours before their true colours are revealed. But I guess some problems are just too big to hide." She stepped away from the door and toward her closet. "I'm glad you're here Sara. Come on, let's get your things unpacked."

We spent the next few days behaving like good little tourists, visiting the famous Liverpool Walker Art Gallery and walking around Liverpool's beautiful port. We also drove to London to visit Buckingham Palace, take a stroll in Greenwich Park and do some shopping at Harrods department store where Lillith helped me pick out the perfect souvenirs for my Mom, Dad and Ali. It was mostly just

Lillith that I spent my time with. The rest of her family always seemed to be off doing something here or there. And after that first evening of my arrival, we never all sat down to dinner together again. Everyone ate at the time that suited his or her own schedule, that's if they came home to eat at all. Sometimes, we caught Lillith's mom as she sat in the kitchen eating dinner alone and joined her. Lillith's father worked late, or at least I assumed he was working, and he rarely made it home on time for dinner, no matter how late we waited up. When he did finally arrive home, he arrived with a bang—and I mean that literally. He would stagger in the front door, throwing his briefcase and keys on the table in the entrance and missing every time. Lillith would beckon me upstairs if I was around to see this, where we would sit in her bedroom with the door locked. If Lillith's mom was awake when her father came home, they would argue for the next hour. If she was asleep, Mr. Burnaby-Green would wake her up so that they could argue for the next hour.

"You've been to the pub again haven't you?" her mother would yell. "Would it be so hard to come home sober for once in your bloody life?"

Lillith was always quick to turn up the television in her room to full volume in an attempt to drown out their hollers. And she and I would sit there, pretending to be interested in the TV show we were staring at, when in reality we were trying hard to ignore the show unfolding beneath us.

One night, as I tried to fall asleep over the racket from downstairs, I remembered something Lillith had said to me when she'd first come to stay with us. She was talking about my family and she'd said: "You're very blessed you know." I remember her pausing for a moment before she continued that thought with: "But somehow I don't think you do know." And for the first time in my life, I realized that maybe Lillith was right. Maybe I didn't know. Maybe just now, as I lay there, thousands of miles away from home, listening to a grown, professional man smash beer bottles on his kitchen floor and throw up all over himself, I was beginning to know. Just now the fog was beginning to lift. Lillith had respected me enough to tell me the truth that night a few years back, but I hadn't been brave enough to hear it.

I put my hands over my ears in an attempt to shut out the noise, but it was no use. Sleep would not come to me this night.

Most days I woke up to the sound of Lillith's parents fighting in their bedroom next door. It was only sleep or work that could temporarily interrupt their feuds.

"I'm sorry about them," Lillith would say.

"Are they okay?" I would ask.

"No, but they've always been like this. Ever since I can remember, things have been this way. Sometimes I actually wonder if they enjoy fighting, if they take pleasure in hurling hurtful words at each other at the top of their lungs. Sometimes I wonder if there is any love left between them."

England was beautiful but its picturesque scenery was overshadowed by the darkness we would come home to after a pleasant day of touring. It was as if a murky shadow hung over the Burnaby-Green residence. And I began to understand why Randy, Lillith's older brother, had gone away for university half way across the world, and why Jay spent most of her days and nights out with her friends. I began to understand why Lillith appreciated my family so much, and for once, I began to truly appreciate it too.

On the plane ride back from England, I didn't get a wink of sleep. My head was too busy spinning around itself. I had so much on my mind. I had seen so much in the past ten days. Too much. Things I had never wanted to see so up close and personal. Things I would never wish upon my worst enemy. I couldn't wait to see my Mom and Dad, to hear their calm voices and feel their soft touch. I was going home, and I couldn't have been more thrilled about that.

After my first year of university and my trip to England, I did a lot of reflecting. Reflecting that led me to come to the decision that I wanted to live at home again while I studied. In fact, I wanted to live at home again for as long as possible. My parents welcomed my decision to move back in with them and promised to make our house a very suitable environment for studying, which it had always been anyway. I began to see that even though my parents were immigrants, they were two of the most well-adjusted people I knew. The things I once resented them for were the things that in fact made them who they were: good people and good parents. And unlike the long-lasting and detrimental effects divorced or alcoholic parents have on their children, my parents' accents when they spoke English was something I eventually learned to ignore; and then something I ultimately learned to embrace and appreciate. It was part of their identity, their history, and that is something no one should be ashamed of. So when my Mom spoke to my friends or teachers without properly pronouncing the p, my adolescent vanity was punctured, but that was about it. I began to see past the exterior shell I had held in high esteem for so long and deep into their core. And there, I saw that my parents had hearts of gold. The more I grew in time and experience, the more my admiration and appreciation for them grew. Their patience, their strength, their values, their wisdom, those were far more important than their words or wardrobes.

Just recently, I cried for the first time since I was a child when my Dad left for one of his routine business trips. As he stood by the door, pulling on his jacket and slipping his plane ticket into his breast pocket, I felt a hard knot forming in my throat. He would only be gone for a week, but that didn't seem to matter to my heart. He leaned in to hug me quickly before the taxi honked for the second time, reminding me to check the mail as he was expecting an impor-tant letter. I nodded and wrapped my arms around him, like a child hugging her favourite teddy bear, and buried my face in his shoulder. I felt my eyes brimming with tears, and my vision became blurred.

And then, before I could stop them, the tears escaped me. One by one they dripped noisily onto his beige jacket until they had formed a dark puddle on his shoulder, staining it with my silent love. My Dad pulled back and looked at me.

"Are you okay Sara?" I could see the mix of concern and confusion in his eyes. A loud honk sounded from the driveway.

"Yes Baba," I blubbered between sniffles. "It's nothing, I'm fine." But I wasn't fine, I was deeply in debt. And at that moment I realized that I would never be able to repay him and my mother for all they had done for me.

My father took my right hand in his and gave it a tight squeeze before picking up his suitcase. He stepped out on the porch to let the taxi driver know he hadn't forgotten him, and then he paused and turned back to me, his fallen daughter, standing there with my pinched face and red eyes.

"Are you sure you're okay honey? I don't have to go." But I knew that wasn't true, for eventually, they would both have to go. We all would. I couldn't hang on to them forever. I nodded weakly, almost imperceptibly and watched as he got into the taxi, slowly, hesitating a bit. The big blue Buick quickly reversed out of the driveway and sped down the street and out of sight.

Though it has been some years since that day, I still remember that feeling vividly. It is a feeling I often walk with now, as I brace the world as a newly married woman, living far away from the place I called home, and far away from the two people who worked so hard to make our house a home, the feeling of absolute appreciation for the two people that put up with so much from me. They were never aware of the fact that I considered myself a fallen daughter. They would never have accepted it if they knew, and I thank God every day that that's the way they were. As I sat at the breakfast table this morning, something took me back to those earlier days when I would wake up for school and stumble down to the kitchen to find my mother humming as she scrambled some eggs. Maybe it was the crisp fall air that my mother loved to feel on her skin. She always had a window cracked open somewhere in the house to allow just enough of it in. Maybe it was the smell of the traditional Moroccan bread baking in the oven. Maybe it was the sunlight streaming through the glass. Whatever it was, it transported me back to a place far away in miles but very very close to my heart.

My mother has always been my therapist. No appointment needed, no hefty bills paid in full by the 15th of every month. No. I would just wander into her bedroom, plop down on her bed and my psychoanalysis would begin. I could trust her with anything as I couldn't imagine someone who loved me more on this planet. In a time when nothing was easy, she made things a little less difficult. Plus, it was always service with a smile, and often, some warm chicken soup too.

Growing up, I believed this was the norm. Believed that all children could come home to the comfort of knowing there would be an attentive ear there waiting for them to cathartically release the day's flood of emotions. My flood gates often opened at 4:00 pm each afternoon. Sometimes, I'd release a flood of words and stories and sometimes, I'd release a flood of tears. But no matter what came flowing out of my mouth or down my face, there was always someone there, listening, nodding, commenting, but most importantly, not scolding or judging. After I'd spoken the last word, or after I had squeezed the last drop from my eye, there was usually gentle feedback waiting for me—ideas, suggestions, brainstorming sessions that we had together.

After getting married and moving away, I lost a part of that— the therapy part. The late-night and early morning discussions that temporal time did not seem to affect were no more. The last-minute words of wisdom that my mother would utter as I slipped on my jacket and ran to catch my bus, the hugs, the squeezes, the inside jokes and made-up songs. But simply: her presence.

At 24, I still sometimes find myself confused without her, how do I respond to this? How do I react to that? And now, getting the answer to these questions seems to be more exhausting than ever. For the first time in my life, I may need to make an appointment, scribbled down in my agenda beside the list of topics I feel the need to discuss. And for the first time, conversations seem unnatural, scripted with a red pen. Hesitant voices span the telephone line.

My mother once asked me if I thought parents should raise their children to have a more distant, formal relationship with them to save them the separation anxiety of having to part for good. I responded with a fervent no, for I am still grateful that I had it once, instead of never having had it at all. I am still grateful for the sweet memories of our tangent-laden conversations that were still more to the point than ever, the point of building closeness and communication. I am still grateful for the shared words that were more than just letters strung together to convey a message. These words conveyed hopes and dreams and love. A blessing is a blessing, even if it only lasts for so long.

I sit in silence some days now, with my thoughts and memories filling the quiet room. I've come to see that life is just a little harder than I once thought it, and especially hard when lived with a lack of vibrant words. I am the anchor now, the source of support that must hold things in place. Tipping left or right shakes more than just my spirit now, it shakes the foundations of a young family of which I am half. I may not always have the knowledge to share but I have the ears to listen.

Without discussion, old doubts linger in my thoughts and mind. The price of sharing these doubts is higher now, no longer just a passing phrase, a momentary hesitation. For if I call long-distance to speak of them, they must be serious. Yet they are only serious because I let myself go for this long without speaking of them. It is a catch 22 at its best.

And so my discussions have turned inwards. I've learned to initiate a conversation with God, for He is always willing to listen. But it is I who is not always willing to ask.

A Nocturnal Plea

In dim light I raise my hands
Arms outstretched
Only One can answer this call
Only One can hear my inaudible whispers deep in the night
Sleepers stir restlessly
It is not in discomfort that I rise now
But in need
Need of Your forgiveness
Need of Your acceptance
Need of Your love
Others may give me what I crave
But it is never enough
Until I give my soul what it craves
And what You wish for me
Purity, Piety, Passion
Both exciting and divine
Given only by the Sublime

Pushing the Pearl Aside

I'll never forget it. I was 13 years old. Me, Maddie, Barbara, Britney and Juliet were standing in a tight circle in the school yard. Eight eyes stared at me in shock, unable to understand the words that had just escaped my mouth.

"So you mean you're never going to kiss someone until you get married?"

"Yeah…" I answered faintly while wondering if my face was on fire.

"Wow. That sucks. So are you ever going to date someone?"

"No, I don't date."

"Why not?"

"Because…because…"

Driiiiiinnnnggggg! Saved by the bell!

I will never forget that conversation, or should I say, confrontation. It was the first time I had to explain that I would never kiss a boy, that I would never date, ultimately, that I would never experience the 'joys' of being a 'real' teenager. Thankfully, junior high passed quickly with few encounters concerning my single status, but this would soon change come high school.

Three years later, I was still friends with the same four girls that questioned me so intently that day on the school yard. Although my friends and I were in grade ten and still shared many of the same likes and dislikes, I knew my 'no dating' status would constantly cast a barrier between me and 'fitting in'. High school was entirely different from junior high; teenagers walked around with an air of arrogance whilst traces of insecurity seeped through their unsure movements: crowded, congested hallways threatened punctuality and cafeterias wreaked the odour of teenage angst. There was no escaping boy-girl relationships, for they popped up at every corner of the school. Girls didn't just dream about boyfriends as in junior high, they had them. Luckily for me, none of my friends had yet succumbed to this adolescent requirement–for now. This meant that most of our week-ends were still spent in the sweet security of girl-like innocence: going to the movies, shopping, eating at restaurants and the odd sleepover. At the movies, we happily asked the cashier at the canteen for 'double the butter' on our popcorn before entering a world of fantasy; at the mall, we memorized the location of our favourite stores; at restaurants, the food ignited within us a feeling of independence; and sleepovers were the best of all, for they offered us a timeless haven of careless enjoyment. Those memories are etched within me, memories that provided temporary solace in the senior years of high school, when such activities became scarce.

"For the announcements today, there will be a bakesale at lunch in room 204, proceeds go to the grade eleven trip to New York in April. And now for the announcement you have all been waiting for: this Friday is the Halloween dance, so wear a costume and get ready for a great time! Admission is 8$. "

"The dance! I'm sooo excited, it's going to be sweet! Are you going to it Mona?" Maddie asked from her seat in front of me. We were in French class and trying to keep ourselves awake.

"Not sure. I still need to ask my parents..."

"Well you better come. My mom said you and the rest of the girls can come to my house before to get ready, and I will need a lot of time to make myself look perfect for Brad!!" Her eyes lit up when uttering the name of her future conquest, a name that had been repeated countless number of times in the past week.

"Are you going to dance with him at the dance?" I asked.

"For sure! There's no way he'll be able to resist my girlish charm! Hey, maybe Corey will be there!"

"Maddie! Be quiet!" I responded quickly.

Corey Sanders: the name of my crush for the past year. Whenever

I heard his name mentioned, I felt my limbs becoming numb, I felt my convictions weaken; his name entered my ears and circled my childish heart, fluttering within me and latching on to each remnant of rationality. Each day I looked forward to standing at my locker where I would see him opening his locker a few steps away. Each time I heard him say "Hey Mona" in the hallway, every other person around me faded into oblivion, and my eyes became fixated even though my insides were crumbling, and I would coolly respond "hey". These were the moments I wished I could date someone, these were the moments I wished I could date Corey.

That night I dreaded bringing up the subject of the dance with my parents. They always seemed to have some kind of objection concerning such activities and I usually pretended not to know why. I figured that dinnertime would be the best time and so I politely looked at my father and asked:

"Daddy, there's a dance on Friday and I need to go because I'm on Student Council and I'm selling tickets at the door."

"Will you be dancing at this dance, or selling tickets the whole time?"

"I'll mostly be sitting at the door."

"Will there be boys at the dance?" My father looked at me with trusting eyes.

"Unfortunately." I answered nonchalantly. "But I'll obviously only be dancing with my friends."

"Okay Mona. But remember that Allah *subhana wa ta'ala* is always watching you, always keep this in mind."

"Thanks Daddy! Is it okay if I get ready at Maddie's house before the dance?"

"Okay, as long as her mother is home."

"Yeah, she will be. Thanks!"

Mission accomplished! I cleaned off my plate and ran to my room to call Maddie and tell her the good news. I could hardly dial her number out of excitement.

"Hello?"

"Maddie! It's Mona. I'm allowed to come to the dance!"

"That's awesome! It's going to be so fun! Me and the other girls were talking and decided we're all going to dress up like the Spice Girls!"

"Really?! Cool! I shotgun being "Sporty" Spice." I exclaimed, remembering that "Sporty Spice" was the most modest out of the five.

"Sorry, she's already taken. Besides, you have to be "Scary" Spice since you look the most like her and you have the coolest hair! I have an awesome outfit you can wear, that may just impress Loverboy!" Maddie exclaimed excitedly.

I shuddered nervously and hoped this 'outfit' was a little different than "Scary" Spice's regular attire.

"Oh, well I guess I'll see it when I come over,"

"Ok, cool. See you tomorrow!"

"Later!"

The next day (which meant the dance was the next day!) I was sitting by my locker catching up on French homework when I heard someone calling my name.

"Hey, Mona!"

I turned around. It was Corey! Did he see the pearls of sweat run down my face? Could he hear my heart beating loudly, chanting his name between each beat? I looked up from my books and replied, "Hey, what's up?"

"Ah, nothing much." He advanced closer and sat beside me on the floor by my locker. My body felt light but I could not help feeling a little guilty at the same time for allowing such a small distance in between us. I shifted my body further away from him.

"So, are you going to the dance tomorrow?" he turned to me and asked.

"Yeah, I guess. Should be fun I guess. Are you?" I tried to give an I-don't-really-care look, but I was afraid it may have turned out to be a please-be-coming look instead.

"Yeah, me and some of the guys are dressing up like the Beatles. And it was NOT my idea, haha."

"Haha, sure it wasn't. Me and my friends are going as the Spice Girls. A little outdated I know, but I must admit, they are still legends." Wow, I was smooth!

"Haha, that's cool. I think some of the Beatles want a little Spice tomorrow."

What was he referring to? What was going on here? I felt my hands get clammy and wondered whether I had been a little too friendly. While I quickly rummaged my brain for possible explanations for this odd comment, Corey interrupted my thoughts.

"Hey, I was talking about Brad. He's pretty crazy about Maddie."

"Haha, yeah I figured." *NOT.*

"So…is Juliet going too?" he asked.

"Yeah, why?"

"Just wondering…anyway, I gotta go. See you tomorrow!" He got up and made his way to the cafeteria.

No! Don't go!

"See ya." My voice trailed off.

Dring Dring! Dring Dring! I rolled over and switched off my alarm clock. I rubbed my eyes and then remembered that today was the dance! Today I would be a Spice Girl and maybe even hang out with the Beatles!

"Mona! Wake up *Habibty*! Breakfeast is ready!"

"Coming Mama!" I jumped out of bed, quickly got dressed and flew downstairs.

"Mona, I made you some eggs and toast. Did you sleep well?"

"Yeah! Thanks Mama, breakfeast looks yummy!"

"*Alhamdulilah.* This is a blessing from God."

Alhamdulilah. Ever since my mind had been consumed by the dance, I had forgotten to mention this word for a while.

My mom took a seat beside me, and while holding her mug of tea, looked sincerely into my eyes.

"So, why must you go to this dance again? Honestly Mona, I think you're getting a little too old for dances. It's not proper for a Muslim girl to be in that kind of atmosphere, boys and girls dancing together. You know that this is looked upon as normal in our society, but it's not. These kinds of activities always lead to other things. And when I came to pick you up last week from school, I was astonished to see what some of your friends were wearing. It's quite saddening."

"Mama! I'm obviously aware of all these things! And I never dance with boys, and I don't dress badly. Besides, I have to go to these dances since I'm on Student Council." Who was I trying to convince? Mama or me?

"Well, just remember what your father said."

"I will." *Allah subhana wa ta'ala is always watching you.*

At school, my morning classes dragged on forever. I could hardly wait until lunchtime so me and my friends could sit and talk about the dance. As soon as my last class finished, I walked briskly down the hall to my locker, where my friends would be. Maddie and Barbara ran to greet me.

"I can't wait for tonight!" Barbara cried between bites from her Turkey sandwich.

Maddie pulled out a container of noodles, grinned and said:

"Yeah, it should be good. And our costumes are going to make it all the better. I cannot wait to show you yours Mona, you're gonna love it."

"Hey Maddie! You better save a few dances for me tonight, eh?"

Maddie quickly turned around to see who had just made this bold statement; it was her precious Brad.

"I'll try but I'm in pretty high demand." she replied smoothly.

Brad playfully flicked her blond ponytail and answered, "I know."

After school was FINALLY finished, me, Barbara, Britney and

Juliet took Maddie's bus to her house. We laughed hysterically on the bus and tried to suppress the anticipation bubbling in the pit of our stomachs. When we reached her house, we prepared ourselves some sandwiches, relaxed in front of the television, and tried to kill some time before we were to get ready for the big night.

"So Mona, if Corey asked you out, would you say yes?" Juliet looked at me with curious eyes.

"No, I told you guys before, I don't date. I can never picture myself being with someone for a little while, and then changing to another guy, and another. It'd be too weird. When I am with someone, it will be special, because he'll be committed, he'll be my husband. Dating is not allowed in Islam, and it makes sense to me. So many problems come from dating."

Britney turned and looked at me. "I get it. Last year when Jake broke up with me, I was about ready to kill myself, haha." Britney looked down, her smile faded and I could see pain in her eyes.

"But why would you go to the dance, if you can't even be with the guy you like?" Juliet asked.

"Cause it's fun!" Maddie interrupted.

But Juliet had asked an important question that reverberated in my ears. What was the point? Why was I going to the dance? How could I justify the tenets of Islam while also defying them at the same time? It's not like Corey liked me, and even if he did, I knew dating was not right. I had seen the negative impact of dating on all my friends: low-self esteem, depression, insecurity. So what was driving me to go?

It'll be fun! I submitted to the voice of my lower self, dismissed my reservations, and convinced myself that I was required to attend the dance for Student Council.

"OK, girls. I think it's time to get ready! The dance starts in 45 minutes. Let's go upstairs." Maddie led the way and we followed. *Maddie led the way and I followed.*

"Ok, Mona. Time for me to show you what you'll be wearing!" Maddie eagerly took me by the hand to her closet. She rummaged through her messy clothes and pulled out a small piece of blue fabric (I was not entirely sure what it was) and some bright red, fake leather pants. She handed them to me, and said:

"So here's your outfit! I got this blue tube top from Le Chateau and the pants a while back....you're going to look phenomenal. Corey won't be able to take his eyes off of you! Go try it on!"

So this blue piece of fabric was supposed to be a shirt! My legs guided me to the washroom and I put the outfit on. The tube top was strapless and showed my midriff, while the pants were rather tight. I looked in the mirror but before my conscience could object to the unfamiliar reflection, Maddie's voice urged me to show her the result. I shyly opened the door and revealed to her *her* creation.

"Wow! You look incredible! This is the first time I have see you in something strapless, you're always covering up your beautiful figure with those loose clothes!"

Juliet, Barbara and Britney entered the room and looked at me in shock. Their faces said it all: I looked different, I looked good! *Allah is always watching you.* I violently pushed the reminder aside; ignored the warnings that echoed in my heart and followed the girls to the car.

When we got to the school, I glided in with superficial confidence and made my way to the ticket booth.

"Wow, Mona, you look so good!" exclaimed Alexandra, the grade nine representative on Student Council.

"Thanks!" I couldn't recognize my own voice.

I handed students their tickets as they fought through the line: Elmo, Dracula, the Three Musketeers, Britney Spears, everyone was here, everyone except Corey. Was he coming? Would he notice my transformation? I uncomfortably tried to pull down my tube top in order to cover my midriff, but the more I pulled it down, the more I felt exposed, and so I pulled it back up. More students walked in: Paris

Hilton (what did Emma think she was wearing?!), Winnie the Pooh, A Witch, Beauty and the Beast, still no sign of Corey. An hour passed, my shift at the ticket booth was almost over when all of a sudden I saw the Beatles strolling in. Brad, Mark, Stuart and Corey; of course they came fashionably late, they needed to make an impression. I stood at the booth and waited for them to approach. Why did I feel so out of place? My heart felt heavy, constricted, as though it was a struggle to keep it in my chest. Was the tube top *that* tight?

Corey approached with the rest of his crew. He was wearing thick, black glasses with a wig, black pants and a black vest; he really did look like one of the Beatles. I looked elsewhere until he made his way to where I was standing.

"Hey, Mona. Looking good!" he exclaimed.

Allah is always watching.

"Thanks." I answered.

He handed me his ticket, smiled and disappeared. I smiled back. I turned to Alexandra and told her my shift was over and made my way into the gym. It was completely dark except for the flashing fluorescent lights and the tacky Halloween decorations. My heart was darkened. I could see bodies swaying hypnotically to the music and vaguely make out the faces of some of my peers. I made my way through the crowd and searched for my friends.

"Mona!!" My friends yelled in unison.

I joined their circle and we danced to "YMCA". It was a fun song to dance to because everyone knew the gestures. People pushed me from all sides, the place was crowded but I could not help feeling out of place. Where was Corey? I looked around and saw him. He was dancing with Nikki Green, she was dressed as Dorothy from the Wizard of Oz. Maybe he would stop dancing with her after this song? "YMCA" finished and "Love Song" blasted from the speakers; the dreaded slow song. I looked to my right, and saw Maddie float off with Brad into deeper darkness. Dale asked Barbara to dance, and

Britney (who had not been asked to dance) asked Timothy herself to prevent humiliation. Was Corey still dancing with Nikki? No. Where was he? There he was! He was approaching me and Juliet, he opened his mouth and I could not believe my ears:

"Juliet, wanna dance?"

"Sure." she held his hand and they drifted away.

Oh, the betrayal of high school romance.

I was standing alone, in the middle of a crowd. The place became blurry. I quickly made my way to the nearest refuge: the change room. I sat on the bench, put my head in my hands and wept. I wept not because Corey had asked Juliet to dance instead of me, but because tonight I had compromised my dignity, I had compromised my religion. I had hungered for the wrong kind of attention. I had dove into the maelstrom of teenage conformity and been spat out mercilessly. I had been rejected by someone I never should have sought in the first place!

I left the dance early, came home and ran to my room so my parents would not see what I was wearing. I threw the clothes into a plastic bag and vowed never to look at them again. I sat on my bed and opened my journal. I had not written in it for a long time, but I needed to now. I could only reveal my shame to the lifeless paper that lay in front of me. I turned the pages and glanced at my last entry, it was dated July 5th, 2006, a little over a year ago. I began to read it.

Dear Diary,

I just came back from a wonderful week at the Muslim Youth of Toronto Camp! I was pretty nervous at first to go but then Mama and Daddy convinced me that I would have a nice time, and be surrounded by Muslims for a change, and so I gave in. It was incredible. Everyday we woke up for fajr and while walking to the mess hall where we would pray, all I could hear were the birds softly singing in praise and the wind's gentle murmur of worship and I knew I was fulfilling my purpose. I loved being there. My heart felt at peace, my mind at rest, and my soul alive. And I also built some real friendships. I need to remember what I have learned here and what has been revived within me! I need to remember that Islam is light and oxygen. It's a precious pearl given to me. I need to hold onto it tightly…if ever I lose my grasp of it, I'll have lost everything.

How had I forgotten this? How had I forgotten the feeling of serenity that had once resonated within me? What was more important to me, to please a boy I liked or to please my Creator?

I grabbed the pen on my dresser, held the diary and began to write:

Dear Diary

Tonight was a night I'll never forget. I tried to impress my friends and I tried to impress Corey. I failed in both respects and ended up humiliating myself.

And what's worse is that Allah SWT placed within me the ability to feel that what I was doing was wrong, but I carelessly pushed aside each warning sign and immersed myself in darkness. I feel so pathetic. I stood there and watched Corey dance with one of my best friends and asked myself how I could have lowered myself to such a level. Only now do I realize that his not asking me to dance was a blessing. Allah protected me from myself.

Islam is the pearl of my heart and never will I push this pearl aside again.

Contradiction

When courage is technology
And love is a greeting card
When beauty is a lipstick bar
And words are very hard

When people punish others
For what they've done themselves
And the rich would rather burn their cash
Then share their filthy wealth

When wars are fought with buttons
And people killed with keys
When fingers do the fighting
And murderers take leave

When true is false
And false is true
When right is wrong
Unless it's you
When nations starve
While others waste
When love is bad
And good is hate

When peace is no longer on the mind
And only a piece will do to grind
The treaties, acts and resolutions
That never bring about solutions

Not on my Watch!

7:30. Fifteen minutes until the school bell rings. Fifteen minutes until I begin a new year in my life.

I couldn't believe it—it was the first day of 9th grade—my freshman year, and my first official year of high school. Though I was disappointed that summer was over, I was anxious to see my friends who had gone on vacation, and see what classes I was taking that year. Because I had been attending what our district called a "choice school," where middle school and high school are in the same building, it meant that I would interact with the same 57 kids I have known and seen everyday since the seventh grade.

My classmates were from all over the globe. Even though I was the only Palestinian in our graduating class, my best friends came from diverse nations and cultures—in other words, though they were all residents of the US, their parents came from different countries and brought with them their respective traditions. Many religions were represented in my graduating class. We were made up of Christians, Jews, Buddhists and I was the only Muslim. Religious differences were not an issue for us and I was the best of friends with several of my Jewish classmates. True, we did have a few debates here and there during the course of the year, but overall we remained good friends. Another plus about my school was that, unlike other high schools where it was difficult for a Muslim girl to wear a hijab, my classmates were very accepting of my decision to do so. In the end everybody learned to respect me for who I was not what was on my head.

As a typical Muslim teenager at school, it was often hard for me to accept the fact that I couldn't attend school dances or socialize with my classmates at all night schooling or out of school camping events. But besides that, I felt like everything was going fine—that is, until we found out that our old International Studies teacher had left the school, and had been replaced with a new one.

I anxiously walked over to the portable for our first advisory of the year, or homeroom period as others may call it. I felt excited; I was sporting a new hijab style and outfit I had bought in Egypt that summer.

"Asiya!" I heard a group of people yelling my name from behind. My four closest friends, Chelsea, Liz, Sarah, and Madi came and embraced me.

"Oh my gosh. Your scarf—it's gorgeous! You look amazing Asiya!" exclaimed my best friend, Sarah. Several other old friends came from behind and jumped all over me. I hadn't seen anybody since last June, so I was naturally the center of attention.

At this point I was super excited. Can I get a better start to a new school year, I thought? Just as I was about to exclaim how excited I was to see everybody again, the bell rang, and it was time to go inside for advisory.

After half an hour in the small portable, meeting up with old friends and catching up on summer news, it was time to get our schedules for the next two semesters. I opened up the slip before me, and noticed the new International Studies' teachers' name—Luke Markus. I breathed a sigh of relief after realizing I had that class, and my other five classes, with a few of my closest friends.

The first couple of hours of the school day went on as any other day—I received my books, my supply lists, and we recounted our summer adventures to our teachers. After an all school assembly, it finally came time for the highly anticipated third period.

As everybody was getting settled into third period International Studies, a tall, bald, and slightly daunting man entered the room. I could have sworn he was at least six and a half feet tall! He was wearing crooked sunglasses and a sweater-vest with the familiar colors red, white, and blue. Everybody was quiet as he approached the podium in front of the white-board.

"Hello class," he began with a slightly intimidating smile. "My name is Mr. Markus, and I will be your International Studies teacher this year," he said. Though everybody was slightly unnerved by his staggering appearance, we thought, what the heck, he seems like a pretty nice guy. When we realized he had no eyebrows, it was all the more interesting.

As the first few weeks of school passed and we settled into the new year, we grew accustomed to Mr. Markus' teaching style. We did little to nothing in that class. He often had power point slides prepared, where he would lecture us on prominent events during the Roman empire while pointing at random pictures he had found when he googled "Roman empire" on the internet. I looked over at Sarah at the other side of the room. She was sleeping. So was the rest of the class, I had noticed. Our classroom reeked of boredom. What the heck, I thought. I put my head down too.

After nearly two months had passed, we had just finished reviewing the expansion of the Roman Empire. By this time, Mr. Markus thought it would be exciting if we integrated some current events into our classes; in other words, every Wednesday would be devoted solely to current events, whether they were about any local news or concerning international affairs.

That week just happened to be the week during which bombings occurred at a wedding in a popular hotel over in Amman, Jordan. The first Wednesday after he had announced his new idea, he came prepared to class with an article from the newspaper, and a few websites he found on the internet, including CNN's.

"Those Islamic Fundamentalists," he started.

Woooooooa there, I thought. Did he just say what I thought he said? Islamic Fundamentalists? This was probably the first time I had actually put my head up in his class.

"You would think they learned that bombing themselves and killing innocent people just isn't the greatest tactic to use," he continued. "I mean, they killed thousands of Christians on 9/11 just a few years ago. And who could forget the bombings in London; but now their own people? The Prophet Muhammed, who we will be discussing later, never enforced killing people from their own faith, though I'm not so sure about other ones."

By this point, I shot my hand up.

I wasn't going to let this guy go on and on with his own opinion on recent actions conducted by Muslims. And I wasn't about to let the twenty six other kids in class get brainwashed with his ideas.

Mr. Markus called on me.

"First of all," I said after building up enough courage to confront him in front of the entire class, "I find...I find you have absolutely NO RIGHT whatsoever to call and refer to Muslims as fundamentalists" I said. By this point, my leg was moving up and down rigorously as my foot tapped hard on the foot rest of the desk in front of me.

Just as he was about to respond, I continued.

"Second...Second, you CANNOT bluntly state that Muslims killed 'thousands of Christians'." Are you trying to reference the crusades or something?"

Mr. Markus knew I was mad.

"Now Asiya, calm down, I didn't mean anything, I'm just presenting primary sources—the facts you see."

Oh my gosh, I thought. Primary sources; I wasn't sure if he was joking or not, but I for one knew that CNN was by no means a primary source.

"Primary sources?!? What primary sources? And what do you know about Prophet Muhammed? What do you mean he was against Muslims killing people of their 'own kind?' Do you mean he enforced killing people of other faiths?"

Mr. Markus was the kind of man that was naturally pale. So I was afraid when I noticed his bald head turn a bright red.

"Now Asiya, don't be putting words into my mouth. I never said anything of that sort. And we will go into discussing Prophet Muhammed later. I am sorry if I offended you in any way; I didn't say you were a fundamentalist, just a few Muslims in the Middle East—you know those in Iran and Afghanistan. Now can we please move on…?"

I sighed, but continued tracking his every move. We went on to discuss a recent amber alert that happened on the highway a few days earlier.

After third period I felt very nauseous. Like some kind of bacteria had entered my stomach. I felt sick. Everyone knew I was in a bad mood. My classmates had known me for three years and knew that when someone messes with Asiya…it isn't good. Sarah approached me.

"It's ok. I mean, he doesn't know better. He's new, remember?"

Whatever I thought. I felt the double standard. With all due respect to all religions, I knew that if anything was ever said about another religion there would be some kind of uproar. But I sucked it up nonetheless. Several classmates could sense I was feeling uneasy the rest of the day, and told me to forget about the incident. And that's exactly what I did.

Apparently, Mr. Markus felt we hadn't had enough discussion about current events the previous day, because the next day, he had another CNN article handout ready for us on each desk as we entered the classroom.

"Failed Suicide Attempt by Elderly Palestinian Woman," I read in bolded letters.

"I thought since so much is going on in the news lately, we should stay focused on Middle Eastern events this week."

Great, I thought. *More time for him to humiliate me.*

"As you can see in the article" he said, "just last night, a Palestinian woman decided to strap explosives onto her body in an attempt to blow herself up. What do you guys think?" he asked the class.

I was appalled.

"Well" said somebody in the back corner. "I was just wondering, is it some kind of ritual, or practice they do there? I am really confused." She paused and looked around. "I mean, why do I keep seeing Muslims blowing themselves up in the news?"

I noticed it was Kirsten, a shy, yet outspoken girl sitting in the far back corner of the classroom.

"I mean, she looks so innocent in the picture, but why do people like her enjoy killing other innocent people?" Her question seemed to be more directed at me than at Mr. Markus.

I was feeling queasy again. Why are these people so ignorant, I thought? Why are they always so one-sided? I had absolutely no idea who to blame now. I began to lose my voice this time, and I had that feeling that if I was to start talking, I would have probably broken out into tears. I felt like Mr. Markus was out to get me, out to get all Muslims. Nonetheless, I had to deal with this question; I cleared my throat.

"That's…that's a good question, Kirsten." In my attempt to sound diplomatic, I came out sounding a little sarcastic instead. "Maybe what we need to ask ourselves is why? Why would anybody feel the need to kill themselves and kill others?

Several kids lifted their heads up from their desks. I heard somebody whisper "there she goes again."

"Has anybody seen the movie Paradise Now?" I asked the class. Paradise Now was a recent film addressing why some Palestinians resorted to killing themselves. I looked around the classroom, but no one raised their hand. Very few people were familiar with the film.

"Well," I felt my voice weakening. "Well, wouldn't you all agree that there are two sides to every story? I feel this article is very biased against the Palestinians." I know for a fact that, unless in self-defense, Islam is against the killing of innocent people, unlike how it is portrayed in the media. And I had a feeling that it obviously wasn't in this woman's nature to go out and become a suicide bomber.

"Hah" said someone sarcastically out loud. It was my former best friend turned enemy, Lauren. "One of my cousins lives in Israel. She tells me she's too scared to even step out onto her doorstep." She glared over at me, knowing full well that I was Palestinian, and continued: "I think all Palestinians are just suicidal."

I had had it. Insulting my religion and my people is one thing, but now tolerating others as they followed suit was too much for me. The queasy feeling in my stomach was now making its way to my head, and trying hard to hold back the tears from running down my cheeks, I fled the classroom. The corridors were empty. I ran in silence. With every step I took, I could hear my hurried steps colliding with the hallway floor, my heart pounding. With every heart beat I felt a surge of emotions course through my body.

I went to where nobody usually is during class—the girls bathroom. I felt lonely, frustrated and sad all at the same time. How could an entire nation of people be stereotyped under one banner? There, standing alone by the sink, I anxiously dug my cell phone out of the bottom of my bag and called my dad.

"What's wrong Asiya? I'm in a meeting right now..." answered my dad.

"Please Baba, please. Just come, just come and pick me up." I had a mix of emotions churning inside of me at that moment, and I just wasn't thinking straight. After I got home and told my parents what had happened, they became just as frustrated.

"We can't let him go on like this," said my mom. "He can't present the material of one news source as facts. School is all about teaching students good research methods and to validate facts before blindly believing them. Students are supposed to be learning open-mindedness and respect. Shouldn't we email the principal or something?"

I knew that was the worst thing that could happen. Imagine, my parents emailing my school principal about a new teacher insulting my religion. If anybody at school found out, they would have probably made fun of me.

"No, no you can't. Let's just wait. I'm sure we aren't going to continue with current events for long..." I answered.

I was right about us not continuing with current events. But it just so happened that we were going into a new unit—the spread of Islam. When Mr. Markus announced that we were going to study the spread of Islam and the Prophet Muhammed (PBUH), I thought to myself, could things get any worse? Imagine, Mr. "Prophet Muhammed enforces the killing of people who aren't Muslim" Markus teaching our class about him? I knew this wasn't going to be good.

And I was right.

Though this time he had tried to keep his facts unbiased and straight to the point, he was unsuccessful. I tried to clarify most of his misconceptions as best I could, but because I wasn't exactly an expert on Islamic history, several kids in my class just went with 'what the book said.' A few days later, however, I felt Mr. Markus crossed the line when he decided to place pictures of Prophet Muhammed (PBUH) on his power point slides.

"Mr. Markus, I don't mean to be rude or anything. It's just that in Islam, it is forbidden to have any display, whether it be a picture or a statue, of Prophet Muhammed."

"Oh really? I guess I learn something new everyday. And I don't mean to be rude or anything, but what does that have to do with what I am discussing now?" He was going over the *hijra*.

I was really mad. Was he trying to mock me, or trying to make me look stupid in front of the class? Of course it had everything to do with what he was discussing now—he had a giant picture of Prophet Muhammed (PBUH) he had found on the internet up on the screen!

"Well, you see, I was hoping you would erase the picture you have of him on the power point," I replied.

"Oh this?" He said pointing at the screen. "I'll get to that later."

He never did.

Even though it was killing me inside how much Mr. Markus had misinterpreted several aspects of Islam and the current events concerning Islam, I tried to keep calm.

The next day Mr. Markus thought he would give us a break from the unit and introduce a new assignment. It was a new project coming up called the National History Day task, during which you devote your entire second semester to a topic revolving around that year's theme: Communication, the Key to Understanding History. This is my chance I thought. In my head, I knew exactly what I was going to do.

Later that night I went home and spent hours and hours on the computer researching. I knew I wanted to—I had to—do something concerning Islam, specifically the legacy of the Prophet Muhammed (PBUH). This is it, I thought. The one time I can go in front of the class, and spend ten uninterrupted minutes showcasing MY primary sources and MY views on Prophet Muhammed (PBUH). This project was the key to clarifying any misconceptions my class, and specifically Mr. Markus, had towards Islam.

I spent endless sleepless nights researching, until I came up with a solid thesis for the assignment. A few days later, it came time for topic proposals.

"Asiya, please come up to the front of the class" said Mr. Markus.

I was anxious. Considering Mr. Markus' bias view toward my religion, I was afraid he would reject my idea. That morning, however, I had prayed and prayed and hoped for the best.

"What have you got for me?" asked Mr. Markus as I walked up to present my project proposal.

"You see, Mr. Markus, I plan on basing my project on the legacy of Prophet Muhammed"

"Yes, yes I see," he said. "Well then, how does it fit with the theme?"

It seemed as though Mr. Markus was trying to come up with ways for me to avoid basing my project on Prophet Muhammed. I got that queasy feeling in my stomach again—that 'why the heck am I even bothering' kind of feeling. However, I stood up straight and went on to explain:

"You see I decided to base my thesis on how he communicated the practices of Islam to improve the living conditions of the Arabian people. So the title of my project would be 'Prophet Muhammed: Communicating the Teachings of Islam to Equalize the People of Arabia."

"Uh-huh. I see. Well, I guess if it fits the theme well, and you've come up with plenty of primary sources, I'm sure it would be okay."

I breathed a sigh of relief. Thanking him, I anxiously left the classroom. This was my chance, I thought. Not a time to mess up.

For the next two months I spent at least two hours a day researching, going to the library, making phone calls, and interviewing local scholars about the Prophet (PBUH)—how peaceful his teachings were and how he helped a population of uncivilized, aimless Arabs become one of the greatest civilizations ever to exist on the planet. Even though the assignment was time consuming, and I often faced various obstacles, my goal to share the amazing history of Prophet Muhammed (PBUH) and the peaceful teachings of my beautiful religion was what kept me going.

After I gathered all my work together, I composed a script addressing everything from Prophet Muhammed's character, to how his teachings helped improve the status of women and slaves, and how Islam in general helped bring and unite a community of beliefs into one *ummah*. I was to present my project by giving an individual performance, where I was to be a woman from the Prophet's time and explain my life story and the situation of those around me.

The morning of the presentation, I was very nervous. I went to bed at two in the morning, but I was so scared that something was wrong, that I needed more practice, or that the script needed more editing that I woke up 30 minutes later and stayed up until it was time to go to school.

As I sat at the table over breakfast I felt like throwing up. I had never been so nervous in my life! I had been preparing for this presentation for over three months! I prayed *salat istikhara*, and my parents wished me the best of luck. I went through my lines one last time with my mom, made sure everything I needed was with me, and headed for school.

The entire car ride there I kept reciting lines in my head. When we finally got to school, Mr. Markus directed me to where I should set up my props on stage. When I looked before me to see how many people were in the audience, I felt my stomach churn. I felt like quitting, giving up. This whole presentation is pointless, I thought to myself. But then I went through my lines one more time, and it hit me. I wasn't up there to get an amazing grade, or to wow my classmates with my performance; I was up there to straighten out all the misconceptions my class had on our beloved Prophet and the teachings of Islam. I knew I had to straighten up and get my head together—after all, I was representing the Prophet's message—and messing up would mess up my initial intentions for this project.

I saw my friends smiling at me from the audience and giving me a thumbs up, and I started.

As I was reciting my script and presenting my performance in front of the audience, I noticed how attentive most of the students were. Some wore looks of amazement on their faces as I was talking about Prophet Muhammed's teachings, and how he promoted equality for women, slaves, and people of all other religions. I was guessing they had just realized how peaceful Islam really was! Their looks made me feel better, and I continued.

At the end of my performance, I could hear the applause of my fellow classmates ringing throughout the room. Someone even started to chant "Asiya, Asiya…" I was amazed at how much people actually enjoyed it. Even Mr. Markus liked it. By the questions I got asked during the question and answer period afterwards, I realized that many were especially surprised at how different the information I presented was from the information Mr. Markus had been presenting all semester.

Two weeks later Mr. Markus handed back the grades we had gotten on our projects. I was anxious. I looked over at the people around me, and they didn't do too well. Then, Mr. Markus handed mine back.

My good friend Chelsea came over to me.

"Asiya, what did you get?" She asked me.

I turned the paper over and there I saw a 96/100 right in the middle of the page! I was so happy I hugged Chelsea. A tear of joy slid down my right cheek. As I wiped it off, Mr. Markus came up to me.

"Asiya, I must say you did a good job on your research and on your presentation. I recommend you take your project beyond school to a competition called The National History Day Competition."

I was beyond words.

"Sure, Mr. Markus...I'd love to!" I responded happily.

After a few edits here and there, I went on to participate in the regional competition. The regional competition was where only people from our part of the state competed. Finalists from this part of the competition went on to compete with finalists from the rest of the state.

I went on to place first out of nearly 100 other competitors at regionals with my project on Prophet Muhammed (PBUH). As I was looking down at my comments sheet from one of the judges, I was thrilled to find that her view on Islam had completely changed.

"With the media, and post 9/11 and all, it has been hard to find some good talk about Prophet Muhammed and Islam. I used to be one of those people who found the word Muslim synonymous to terrorist. Thanks to your dedication to your topic and the straightforwardness of your presentation, that's changed. Thank you." I read over the comment on the bottom of the page again and again. That was what I was trying to achieve. That comment alone made me feel like I had already won the competition.

From my experiences with my presentation both at school and at the regional competition, I went on and presented my performance confidently. Because of the tough competition, I wasn't a finalist and placed seventh in the state competition. This meant I didn't get to compete at the national level at Washington DC. But even though I lost, I felt I had won the grand prize. Imagine all those people whose perception about Islam had changed. Remembering back to the anxiety and humiliation I had felt for days on end as Mr. Markus went on and on teaching misconceptions about Islam, I now began to see the benefit of those feelings. I feel that Allah gave me the opportunity to experience Mr. Markus' condescending attitude towards my religion so that I would be moved to go out and do this project and so that others wouldn't have the same mindset.

It was exhilarating when I came to school the next week and a mob of kids from my class came and jumped all over me, congratulating me on my win, and supporting my cause.

Sarah and Chelsea came up to me.

"Ahh," said Chelsea. "I literally screamed out loud when I heard you won first at regionals! Congratulations!"

She jokingly hit me on the arm. More people came and embraced me.

Days later, we all received our yearbooks, and it was almost time to say goodbye for the summer. I was touched to find that my classmates wrote such supportive yearbook comments. One girl even asked in my yearbook who would clarify the misconceptions to future kids in Mr. Markus' upcoming classes. I laughed when I read it. But I hoped that Mr. Markus himself had learned something this year and that there wouldn't be as many misconceptions to clear up in future years.

And with that my first official year of high school came to an end.

Though it wasn't easy, I wouldn't have it any other way. I couldn't just sit by and ask "what difference will I really make?", because I could make a difference. And I did.

Memories

Memories are like bubbles that pop when you try to hold them
Pop when you try to relive them
I remember my childhood brimming with red roses
I remember not knowing the pain of life
And death
Pain was the bee that stung me in the foot
Or the time I fell off the swing onto the sand beneath
Tears rolled down my cheeks as I pulled myself up
Jumpers and hair covered in sand
Now I cry for lost brethren and waged wars
Now I cry for real and not for attention
Cry alone at night beneath my covers
Hoping the soft cloth will stifle the noise and soak up the tears
But the next day, I am given the chance to build more memories
Bricks of recollection that construct an existence
I will always have them, they will always be my own
Stored away in the volt within me
Or displayed in a picture frame in my living room
I remember so that I may go on
Remember those who deserve to be remembered
With their valor and grit in the face of adversity
Wielding the past to learn for the present
I remember the memories

Friends

There was a time in my life when my friends were my life. I surrounded myself with them, enveloped myself in their parties and outings, never missing a ski trip, shopping trip or a chat at the café. I couldn't imagine a Friday evening without them. I needed their chitchat, their latest news, and their gossip. Alone in my bedroom at night, after my last friend had left my house, I would plan our next excursion in my mind, even if it was only to the local coffee shop. I was rarely ever alone with my own thoughts, for I rarely allowed it. If the television wasn't humming in the background, then I made sure the radio was on in the periphery. Between music, school, work, and friends I didn't have time for my thoughts. They were usually a bother anyway, nagging me with feelings of anxiety and discomfort, if I allowed them to surface too often. And so I suppressed them, pressed them down into oblivion, drowned them out with the noise I had learned to plant in my life. Silence allowed my thoughts to stir, and that, I felt could not be a good thing. My friends and I connected on so many levels, I told myself. They understood my taste in clothes, movies, music and even food; we just shared so much in common. I blindly overlooked the fact that the things on which we connected so deeply were all frivolous, trivial matters. It's easy to deeply connect on issues that are shallow in nature. But it wasn't my friends I was running to, it was myself I was running from.

I'm not quite sure when or how it happened, but at some point, I realized that Marwa Fareed and I were very becoming very close. She hadn't always been my very best friend in the whole wide world. We'd never done the pinkie swear in grade school or achieved the status of "blood sisters" in junior high, but we were pretty tight. And we seemed to be getting closer and closer each passing year. We started off as classmates in elementary school, and by our senior year in high school, we thought we were soul mates.

When I first met Marwa, we were two little rosy-cheeked, poofy-haired Arab kids in grade two. I had forgotten my lunch box on the school bus, being the absentminded, seven year-old that I was, and Marwa had so kindly offered me half of her *baba-ghanoush* sandwich, delicately wrapped in pita bread. I must have been the only other student in the school who knew what *baba-ghanoush* was, let alone would agree to eat the light brown mush in a sandwich from an almost complete stranger. The sandwich satisfied my growling stomach, but more importantly, the seed of a friendship was planted. But we didn't water that seed for a long time. In fact, Marwa and I remained casual acquaintances for many years until grade seven when we both joined the girl's field hockey team. That's when the seed of friendship planted so long ago began to blossom.

It was in the second semester of our grade 11 year that Marwa and I decided to make a pact. It's a dog eat dog world, we agreed, and the least we could do was stick up for each other. During that year, a series of events had taken place that made us come to the realization that the world could be a mean and nasty place. Roger Crutchett, a student in grade 10, was severely bullied. Marwa and I knew the quiet Roger from junior-high school when he was in our homeroom class in grade eight. Roger failed grade nine and was set back a year. The rest of his life seemed to be going backwards too. Roger committed suicide in February. In the suicide note he left his mother, he wrote that he just couldn't take it anymore. Dog eat dog world was right.

After that, Marwa and I promised that we wouldn't desert each other during our most trying moments. After that, I remember trying very hard to make sure that, no matter what happened, Marwa and I remained on good terms, since we had a pact. I sacrificed a lot for her, sometimes too much. But whenever I felt that our friendship was costing me dearly, I reminded myself of our pact. *It was worth it*, I'd convince myself, *because now she'll cover my back.*

But boy was I wrong.

Humans have a way of seeing only what they want to see sometimes, even if something else is staring them straight in the face. And I failed to see all the signs that were telling me that Marwa and I were taking two different paths in life. We would share a long stretch of road on our journeys, but when we would come upon a fork in the road, we would ultimately split and each one of us would go in a different direction. It was only as I got closer to her that I began to realize how far apart Marwa and I really were.

My senior year of high school was the most difficult year of my life. It was also the most enlightening. Other than the normal stresses any senior student faces, like the stress of picking the right program of study and the right university at which to study it, followed by the long and tedious university application process, I was feeling an additional stress that year. The stress of watching some of my closest friends slowly slip away from me, and the surprise of watching myself not too eagerly try to hold on to them.

It started off in the usual way, with small disagreements between Marwa and I on how best to spend our time. We were a group of about four girls that did virtually everything together or in some combination with each other. Marwa and I were the closest two, with Reema and Lisa joining us whenever they could, which became more and more often as time went on. Our lives consisted of studying hard throughout the week and socializing with each other on weekends. And because it was our senior year, where our marks would really matter, we said we'd put a little more emphasis on studying for the time being; 'said' being the operative word in that phrase. We had always maintained strong academic records and we were determined to go out of high school with a bang and enter university with ease. But determination proved to be insufficient. Something happened: we got distracted with all the freedom our seniority was granting us. It was Lisa who first came up with the idea of skipping English class. A new movie had just opened and she thought we'd have a grand old time at the matinee grand release. We debated it over lunch, "Come on guys," she pleaded, "Not like we'll really be missing anything in English anyway. I mean, really, who hasn't read King Lear like three times already? Besides, Shakespeare is all the same. Can anyone say predictable? They're all going to die in the end anyway, we all know that!" We agreed that she did have a point. And besides it was only one English class. So it was settled, after lunch, we headed to our lockers and packed up for the day. We hopped on the subway and headed to the cinema and I must admit we had a good time.

But what began as an exception soon became a habit, and three weeks later, Reema suggested we pass on the literary discussion of the apparent similitude between George Orwell's *Nineteen Eighty Four* and our present society, for the more exciting alternative: a movie that was taking our present society by storm.

We soon began to pride ourselves on our movie-going and café-chatting abilities until weekends alone were not long enough to satisfy our socializing wants. We considered ourselves intellectual socialites. At first, our parents did not seem to even notice our new habit so long as our grades didn't drop. And though it took more time and effort, I worked hard to make absolute sure that my grades would not be effected by our new lifestyle. But though my grades didn't suffer, other things did. My life began to be so wholly consumed with friends and studying, that I literally didn't have time for anything else. Sometimes, that meant sleep, sometimes that meant my family. I rarely spent time with my family anymore. My mother joked that I would forget what she looked like if I didn't stop studying so hard. I wonder now if that was in fact just a joke or if there was a hint of truth in her cheerful voice. When I would come home from school, I would lock myself in my room and study until dinner time when I would ask my mom to bring my dinner up to my room because I just couldn't spare the time to sit at the dinner table and eat with my family like a normal human being. But on the weekends, I could spare all the time in the world to go out with my friends. House chores became a near impossibility, and my sweet mother, thinking that I was direly pressed for time due to the increased academic workload that came with my grade level, would get down on her hands and knees and do my chores for me. She also told my father not to bother me with any chores and tasks. Couldn't he see how busy I was, she would ask? I didn't bother to clarify exactly how I was spending my time, using her assumptions to my advantage. And I, in my selfish state, believing that my parents were created to serve me and I was created to do well in school and have a good time with my friends, either didn't feel the guilt or pushed it down very deep until I had forgotten that it was there for a reason.

After overcoming the hurdle of university applications in November, the next big challenge that awaited us was a board wide examination that all graduating students had to write in January. The exam would contain sections from a few main subjects. We attended a special class for graduating students only, to help us prepare for the imminent exam. The marks from this exam would be sent to the universities we applied for and would help them determine if we deserved to be accepted into university or not. We awaited the exam in fear. But apparently, not enough fear. What can only be termed stupidity struck my friends the day before the exam, when they actually chose to go see a newly released movie instead of studying in those few and precious remaining hours. I guess old habits just die hard. And at that point, it had, in fact, become a very old habit.

Reema called me on Sunday afternoon, the day before the exam: "Hey Sal, what ya doing tonight?"

"What do you mean what am I doing tonight, have you forgotten what we're doing tomorrow?" I questioned.

"Oh come on," she retorted, "We've only already put in like 5 million hours studying for this exam! I think it would be okay if we took a night off and went to…wait for it…*Cleveland Walks*. It comes out tonight, and I have got to be the first person to see Gusto Maverick in action. Meet us at 7 in front of the popcorn stand?"

"Reema, I know we've studied a lot for this exam already but that doesn't mean we've covered everything. What about memorizing all those equations? What about the third practice test that we didn't do yet? Why don't we postpone the movie until tomorrow and tonight you can all come over and study at my place?

"Thanks hon, but I'm through studying for this one. I couldn't cram any more info in my mind if I wanted to. Enjoy your little solo study session. And if you change your mind you know where to find us."

As much as I wanted to tell Reema that she was making a big mistake, I knew there was no point in arguing with her highness Queen lawyer Reema. Being a good arguer is not always a good thing. Of course, Reema would argue that it is not always a bad thing either.

As soon as I hung up with Reema, I had the temptation to call her back and tell her I had changed my mind. After all, I had been studying really hard for the past few days and could have used a break. But I fought the temptation and resisted reaching out for the receiver. A few more hours of studying wouldn't kill me, but they could mean the difference between an A and a B on this exam. When I finally did allow myself to reach for the receiver, I picked up the phone to call Marwa; I needed some moral support. What I would get would be anything but that.

"Marwa, can you believe it, the girls wanna go see *Cleveland Walks* tonight of all nights!"

"What's so weird about that?" Marwa asked.

"Well, nothing, except for the little fact that we have an extremely important board wide exam that could determine the rest of our future tomorrow at 9:30 am!"

"Salwa," she sighed, "I think you're taking this exam a little too seriously. We're not actually in university yet remember, so why are you already playing the role? Besides, we could all use a break and there's no time like the present."

"Marwa, listen to yourself. Are you actually going to sacrifice the last few hours we have to prep for this thing to go to a movie that will still be playing in theatres everywhere tomorrow? I don't know about you but I still haven't memorized those ridiculous equations or done the last practice test."

"Thanks Salwa, but I'll figure it out. Right now, I need a break."

"Your choice," I muttered, *and what a stupid choice it is*, I thought to myself.

I tried to forget about our little quarrel and focus on the pile of review papers in front of me. Among all the subjects on the exam, I knew that the calculus questions would be my ultimate demise. So when I wasn't thinking about what my friends were up to, I spent the good part of my study time learning and relearning difficult equations that just didn't want to stick. My mother kept popping into my room offering to bring me whatever food my little heart desired. But my little heart only desired to get this thing over with so I could go on living my life and enjoying my time with my friends.

I remember the day of the exam like it was yesterday (which could have something to do with the fact that after it all happened, I played out the events of that day in my mind time after time). I forced myself to eat the egg sandwich my mother had stuffed in my backpack as I rode the subway to school. Between bites, I would close my eyes and picture the various equations I had stayed up all night memorizing. I felt like numbers were spewing out of my ears. I would conquer calculus, I convinced myself. I would grab it by the horns and shake it wildly until there was nothing left to fear. I knew I had studied well and done all that could possibly be done to prepare. I would ace this exam.

Though I was feeling somewhat more calm and confident by the time I was shoved off the subway in typical New York style, my clammy hands and pulsing heart persisted. As I treaded to the gymnasium where the final exam would be held, I caught a glimpse of Marwa and the other girls huddled together beside the vending machines, whispering secretively amongst themselves. I decided I'd put our differences behind us and act completely normal toward them. I approached the group.

"Hey guys, what's up? All set for this horror show...I must have been up all night just trying to learn those eq..."

"Don't worry, we have a plan," Reema interrupted slyly. She motioned with her head to a tightly folded little paper she had tucked into her sleeve. I got a bad feeling in the pit of my stomach. My heart began to beat faster and my sweaty palms were acting more like a tropical island in monsoon season. I focused all my attention on keeping my egg sandwich down. A look of puzzlement must have been apparent on my face because Reema looked at me and said: "Oh, don't give me that, it's no big deal, miss goody two shoes!"

Marwa and I locked eyes for a moment; she looked away. In my heart, I sincerely hoped that I had misunderstood their plan. I looked at my watch; it was 9:22 am. The exam proctors began to beckon us into the gymnasium; we took our seats in silence. *Bismillah*, I breathed deeply as I flipped open my exam booklet.

What happened after that was like a dream, or rather, like a horrible nightmare. I remember being so absorbed in the exam that I didn't hear or see anything around me. I was on the second last page of the five-page exam when I finally snapped out of my focused trance to hear some commotion erupting in the hallway. The gymnasium door flew open and the principal and vice principal, along with two other people I didn't recognize, marched in. They wore very unsympathetic expressions on their faces. *What in the world was going on?* But before I could figure out the answer to that question, it was tossed in my lap...quite literally; I felt something fall in my lap. I looked down to see a tightly folded piece of paper resting on my left thigh. The paper had scribbles of black pen all over it, but in my daze, I couldn't make out what it said. I looked up and around in absolute confusion, the gym was suddenly very quiet and everyone in my vicinity was looking down at their exam papers, diligently writing away. Out of the corner of my left eye, I could see movement, growing figures that advanced toward me and loomed over my desk. Mr. Walkenger, the principal, Mrs. Riesen, the vice-principal and two other stern-looking strangers looked down at me in utter disapproval. Mrs. Riesen removed the tightly folded piece of paper from my lap and slowly began to unfold it. Time stood still, and then it moved all too quickly. They hauled me out of my desk and dragged me to the principal's office; I staggered alongside of them to keep up. In the principal's office, I sat in a chair across from Mr. Walkenger's desk. The other three interrogators returned to the exam hall to continue their search.

Mr. Walkenger stared at me, the expression on his face dripping with consternation.

After a long silence, he finally spoke: "Do you realize what you've done?" I stared blankly back at him. I must have looked like the world's biggest idiot sitting there vacantly looking into his fiery eyes. I still could not comprehend what had happened. My mind was racing a mile a minute and crawling as slowly as a turtle at the same time. I sat quietly for some time before remembering that he was still waiting for me to answer his question. All I could muster up was: "I...I...I wouldn't cheat. I studied really hard for this exam. Someone is blaming me for their stupidity." My voice trailed off. I sounded about as unconvincing as a kid caught with her hand in the cookie jar.

"Well I'm sorry but you were caught red-handed. And unless someone else comes forward with information that excuses you, we have no choice but to follow what the evidence tells us."

Mr. Walkenger stood up, walked to the filing cabinet at the corner of his office and pulled out my file. "Salwa Badeer," he muttered. He flipped through my file carefully.

"Very unfortunate," he muttered again, "you have a relatively good academic record Ms. Badeer, but I'm afraid that's going to change. If no new information is obtained about this cheating case, then I have no choice but to report that you cheated on your permanent transcript."

My heart sunk. *How would this affect my university applications?*

"You'll also face a two week suspension and have to redo the entire course in the summer."

My heart sunk even lower as tears began to well up in my eyes. *This just couldn't be happening,* I thought to myself. Mr. Walkenger looked at me awkwardly as I brought my thumb and forefinger together in an effort to pinch myself.

"Why don't I call your parents to come pick you up now," he said.

And so my senior year took a drastic turn for the worse. The administration of the school investigated the cheating incident for two entire weeks, but couldn't find any evidence to suggest that I was being framed. As the investigation drew to a close and the last stone had been turned, I still could not believe this was happening to me. As fate unfolded right before my very eyes, I was desperately trying to fold it right back up again and even out the creases in the fabric of my life. For the two weeks of my suspension I had sat at home harbouring feelings of self-pity, shame, hate and just pure anger, until I finally decided to do something. I picked up the phone and dialed Marwa's telephone number, a familiar number which I had not dialed in what seemed like forever.

"Hello," I heard her say.

"Marwa, hi," I replied. I maintained a composed voice though I could feel the anger begin boiling inside of me.

"Oh hi Salwa, how are you?" I couldn't believe how nonchalant she sounded. The coolness on her lips lit a blaze in my heart. Seeing as I wasn't exactly in the mood for small talk, I got straight to the point.

"Marwa, how could you let them do this to me? You know I was up all night studying for that exam and you know I wouldn't cheat. You know this! So how could you just sit by and watch me get blamed for someone else's…irresponsible stupidity? I warned you guys…don't pretend I never told you guys not to go to that stupid movie the night before a board-wide exam. But you idiots made a choice. Why should I have to pay the price for your stupid stupid choice?" As the words emerged from my mouth, I felt a sense of relief. Though I'd never talked to Marwa like this before, it all needed to be said.

"Calm down Salwa. I'm sorry, but I don't know what you're talking about….I'm sorry, but I can't help you."

"You know Marwa, I thought I knew you…I thought I knew you, but either I was deceived or you've really changed, and not for the better."

"I'm sorry," she said again, "I've gotta go". The dial tone rang in my ear. I hung up the receiver and threw myself back on my bed. Just like that, she'd broken our pact, with no regard whatsoever for the weight of one's word. That was the last time Marwa and I spoke. Though for a long time I missed her, I knew that what I really missed was the memory of our friendship. The Marwa I knew and loved was gone. Reacting to all injustices, big or small, with the same nonchalant shrug of your shoulders means that something inside of you has died…something that should be alive and pumping. When you reach a point where no matter what happens, you're okay with it, it's not okay. Standing up for your beliefs doesn't mean allowing yourself to be angered by every transgression big or small, it means doing what you can to change that transgression, even if it's simply by denouncing it in your heart. But Marwa wouldn't even give me that.

After our phone call that night, I cried until I exhausted my tears. And for many months after that I would sometimes just find myself crying at the oddest times. Sometimes you just need to cry. About nothing, about everything. That's the way this life is, and that's why I now choose to live for the next.

I spent a lot of time resenting my once very dear friend. I resented her bitterly throughout the two months of summer school that bored me to death with a subject I'd already learned inside out. I resented her as I sat on the half hour bus ride to and from school and as I got up at

6:30 am everyday while the world slept lazily on in the summer heat.

But only after I'd gone through a period of deep resentment and anger toward her did I realize that it was only a matter of time before Marwa would betray me and break our pact, because the nature of the pact was that it must be broken. And it would be broken, someday, even if not in this life. In the end, it would be broken when I needed it the most, if not in this life then in the next. I realize now that that pact could never have endured, since we would both flee like flies from each other on the day we need each other most: the day of judgment. But at the time, I really believed our pact meant something. And at the time, I naively believed that there was nothing wrong with putting my fate in the hands of a fellow human.

That same summer, I also spent a lot of time feeling terribly lonely. The sudden lack of close friends in my life left a massive void that I yearned to fill somehow. I wasn't used to being alone with myself so often. In short, I had a big problem on my hands: I needed new friends. But this time, I would be a little wiser in choosing them. One of the girls I met in summer school, who was taking the course to get ahead in her studies, asked me once if I'd like to join her at the nursing home she volunteered at after class. I was hesitant at first. My idea of fun was shopping and watching movies, not talking to some oldies trapped in an institution. But out of my desperation to not be alone, I agreed to go with her once to try it out. To my great surprise, I actually enjoyed myself. It felt good to be doing something for someone else for a change. Friendship, I began to see, could revolve around something other than my instant pleasure. That summer brought a few more surprises. I think I surprised myself most when I allowed myself to be alone with me, just me.

It was sometime later that I remembered back to a hot afternoon in Beirut one summer a few years ago. We were lounging around in my aunt's living room, sucking on ice cubes and desperately trying to keep ourselves cool. The T.V. murmured in the background. My aunt had the channel set to a religious program that she liked to watch each day at noon. I had become very good at tuning these things out and usually enlisted the help of my MP3 player that I kept plugged in my ears to drown out the world. But that afternoon, I was feeling especially lazy—too lazy to reach for my MP3 player that was sprawled on the long coffee table in the middle of the room. I lay with my legs outstretched on the couch, body facing the rotating fan, and let the words pass through one ear and out the other. The man on the screen was quoting a saying of the Prophet Mohamed, Peace be upon him. At the time, the saying didn't mean much to me. I later looked that saying up again to remind myself of the meaning. It went like this: "Three things follow a deceased person to his grave: members of his family, his possessions, and his deeds. Two of them return and one stays with him. His family and wealth return and only his deeds remain with him." When I first heard that saying, the profound advice embedded within it was lost on me. But now, with my experiences as living proof, it all makes sense, too much sense. Friends should be ranked based on what they inspire within you. If a friend inspires you to do good, then the fruits of that friendship will be eternal, as these good deeds will follow you to your grave. Otherwise, friendships end at the grave, that is, if they even last that long.

I still sometimes think back to those difficult days in high school, and while I know that millions of humans across time and space have suffered much more injustice than what I faced that year, that knowledge somehow doesn't lessen my pain. But if that incident brought me closer to Allah *subhaba wa ta'ala*, then something good has come of it. Something worth the months of loneliness and an aching heart.

They say a picture tells a thousand words, but often, it tells a thousand lies. When I look through my old photo albums these days, I see through the smiling faces and giggling eyes. I see now that not all friendships are created equal. A friendship is only as strong as what unites the friends. If my friendships are all based on hanging out, and the latest fashions, then I shouldn't be surprised when they wither away like an old fad. But if my friendships are based on something deeper and more profound, then I can expect them to last longer and be more fulfilling. If they are not limited to this life but extend to cover this life and the next, they are guaranteed to last forever. Most of all, if my friendships are based on defying God and his laws, then they are not friendships at all. I still hope to find that perfect friend someday. Not the one that agrees with everything I say and do or enjoys the exact same activities as me, but the one who reminds me who I really am and helps me become a better person. The one who leaves me being proud of who I am even when I'm all alone in my bedroom at night.

If life were a painting, I would paint over certain people in my life. I might paint them as trees, tall and unobtrusive. Or I might paint a flowerbed in their place, something beautiful to cover up the hurt they caused. But life is not a painting. Life is a test, and in this life, I do not hold the master paintbrush in my hands. So I must trust that God brought Marwa and others into my life for a greater purpose. A greater purpose whose wisdom I do not always immediately comprehend. One piece of wisdom that I did walk away with is that at the end of the day, regardless of who is in my life or what circumstances I'm in, nothing is more important than Allah's contentment because in the end, He alone is going to judge me. And He is going to judge me alone.

A lot can change in four years, when I look back now, I sometimes don't even believe I'm the same person that marched into my high school, proud and excited, a mere four years earlier. Some people at my school were complete messes at the time of graduation. Tears streaming down their faces like there was no tomorrow. I was not one of those people. Parting from my friends was neither sweet nor sorrowful—it just was.

My Prophet (SAAW)

I think of you…
Peace be on you.
I think of you…
Of your beauty, your kindness, your sweet strength, your devotion,
Your aura.
Your being.

    I long to be with you.
    To gaze at your luminous exterior,
    And witness your brilliant interior

Thinking of you…

    My palpitating heart is clothed in mercy
    And my thoughts are sweet,
    And my faith is pure,
    And my feet follow you're dignified strides
    My eyes look ahead…

On a Path, in an enchantment of beauty
I strive to follow you're dignified strides
Groves of love surround this path
As I follow you
I extol His Majesty for giving me this benediction

    I remain on the path, following you're dignified strides
    Frequently I plunder
    Torn asunder
    Tangled by unforgiving boughs
    Still…

I keep on my trek, sheltered by your shade
Forcefully, hungrily searching for the glade

As long as I can see your calm silhouette
And hear your devotional antiphonies
As long as the zephyrs worship the Almighty
And plead with me to do the same
And I am reminded of your undaunted courage, I can
Remain on the path

And so I keep walking,
Sometimes running
Sometimes pushed
Sometimes pulled back
Tired of falling but...

One sentence keeps me from being marred
And protects me from being scarred

One Sweet sentence revives my dying heart
One perfect tune reverberates in my ears

"A beloved will be with his beloved".

I pray...let this be my end.

...But we never walk alone

The term *walking down memory lane*, I have found, can be deceivingly casual. When I was initially approached to revisit my younger years and the trials I went through I originally thought this would be a wonderful idea! I'll be able to do a little self-examining, see how much I've grown, write an articulate and moving piece and move right along. It is here that this casual stroll through my teenage years resulted in heart palpitations. I started to have a strange out of body experience and began viewing my younger self as a separate entity that I sometimes wanted to knock upside the head, other times couldn't help blushing for, and most times just shook my head at. But at no point did I not love her and I don't mean love in terms of ego, but rather in terms of tenderness and compassion. I feel for the younger me who was struggling to find herself. The girl who was painfully uncertain at times and who in her heart wanted to be a good person. And maybe it's easy for me to sympathize for her since many of the struggles she had are struggles I continue to deal with today.

One I particularly labor with is being kind for no other reason except for Allah's sake yet balancing this with a healthy self-esteem. We've all been in a situation where someone has been rude to us and speaking personally it's sometimes difficult for me to remind myself that we're not told to only exchange kindness for kindness but rather we're told to be kind to everyone. Trying to strike a balance between this ideal while not subjecting myself to being someone's doormat is a balancing act I have yet to perfect. However as Muslims we are well aware that the sweetness of faith does not lie solely in the perfecting of it but in the struggle of it.

And it must be said that I struggled, and not always so sweetly, with finding a topic to write about for this piece. While trying to fish for ideas for my story, I spoke with many friends and found, surprisingly, that many had completely written off their younger selves, saying, "I was a bad Muslim" or similar phrases of disdain and disregard. But also offering hope by letting me know that my past self, aka: bad, dirty, lowly, little mini-me, could help so many going through similar situations.

"Tell them your experience of being a girl stuck between two worlds," I was told. But to be honest I never felt a trial between my identity: others did. During my teenage years I was too "Canadian-ized" for many Arabs and my Islam was sometimes seen as being a downer in the eyes of many non-Muslims. I distinctly remember being referred to as "white" and being asked why I was attending a peace rally for the Middle East while alternatively I was also faced with the all too typical, "come out and drink with us tonight, we won't tell anyone."

As a teenager I can recall many times when I felt more accepted by non-Muslims than by Muslims. People with the best of intentions can come across as judgmental when giving critical advice. Looking back now I can appreciate how some were just trying to help me out and do what they felt was best for me but at the time I found it challeng-ing to find a safe haven for which I could truly be myself. I felt scrutinized by my Muslim friends who I felt judged me for going to coffee shops downtown, for staying out later than they were allowed, for having more freedom than they had, for only being able to speak English…and the list goes on and on. And my non-Muslim friends never concerned themselves with those issues. So naturally I felt more secure in front of them because I didn't feel as if I was under some sort of microscope. Reviewing this stage in my life has made me realize that although their approach or delivery wasn't always correct, having friends who questioned who I was and why I did the things I did made me a much more well-rounded and contemplative individual. There's nothing wrong with being challenged and as Muslims we should really welcome these situations because critical analysis no matter where or who it comes from can always be a positive thing. So yes I can admit that this time during my teenage years was tough but it definitely wasn't enough to warrant an identity crisis.

"Okay well tell them about how you grew up in this society with alcohol around you and how difficult that must have been," someone recommended. But to be honest alcohol was never a struggle for me. However there is an important point to be made here and that is, everyone's weaknesses though different, are difficult and we cannot assume otherwise. How many times have we looked at others and said, "She never seems to miss *Fajr*, and I always do!" or "He always lowers his gaze so easily around women, why can't I?" This is *shaytan's* playground and the jungle gym is created out of despair. Make no mistake, just because you are struggling with something that your friends are not does not mean that they aren't struggling with something equally painful and difficult. And I'm not sharing this thought so that it may be used as a comforter but rather as an equalizer.

Trust me, there are many events in my past which if I could go back, I would erase. I know the politically correct Miss America answer is, "I believe everything that has happened in my past has led me to this very moment and so if I could go back I would not change a thing." But my Miss Muslim answer is, "heck yeah I'd go back!" And unlike Miss America, I would not go back and hold my former self and let her know it's all going to be okay. No. My Miss Muslim self would march up to my younger self and give her what in the Arab world is commonly known as a *kef* and I'd tell her to sit up and fly straight.

But I cannot go back and so in life we must all serve as an example or a severe warning. And so here I am warning all of you that an ounce of prevention is worth a pound of cure. I sit here tempted to share all the expressions you've heard a thousand times over. Don't Just Do It (Insert swoosh here)! Respect your parents! Visit your family! Speak your mind! Think before you act! Don't be ashamed of who you are! Don't hide your relationship with Allah from those in your life! But you probably won't listen. And the younger me probably wouldn't have either. And not unlike my younger self, you and your younger self will learn but I hope that in the end you will not sever off ties with one another.

So will there be a moment when we'll be able to say as J-Lo so ungrammatically put it, 'This is me, then'? Will there be a defining moment for all of us? A clear fork in the road forcing us to take a path? Well for me it was when I began wearing *hijab* but before you roll your eyes and mouth the word 'typical' let me explain why. Firstly I must say to the horror of some that me before *hijab* is not completely dissimilar from me with *hijab*. I didn't don the *hijab* and all of a sudden a muzzle too by becoming all meek and silent. I was still the same girl. The same girl with the loud laugh, the same girl that loves to have fun, joke around and be social and most importantly, the same girl with the strong opinions. Because lets be honest a piece of cotton doesn't change you and that is all a *hijab* is if you can't realize the significance of the meaning behind it. I didn't look at the *hijab* as a separate entity from myself, quite the contrary, in fact when I put it on I felt it was more an extension of who I was. I finally felt that I was (quite literally) wearing my heart on my sleeve.

However when I put on the *hijab* I knew I would be altering my life and as anyone knows with alterations, you have to be careful because if you pull the wrong string the whole thing could come undone. Not to be melodramatic but at the time it really did feel like my world was unraveling. The individuals who I thought would support me didn't. I had now become too uptight for some while still bearing the burden of those who insisted on letting me know that my *hijab* wasn't 'proper'. All of this was a lot to take. And although no one warned me of this, it was stressful to randomly run into people who had known me pre-scarf because I was worried they would think I had morphed into some fanatical zealot. So needless to say walking into work on Tuesday with a *hijab* on when I wasn't wearing one on Monday was, well in the words of Ricky Ricardo, I had some 'splainin' to do! Luckily everyone at work seemed really supportive which came as such a relief because for better or for worse it was really important for me to have the support of absolutely everyone around me and except for the aforementioned, I thought I had.

Well a year later I ended up bumping into an old employee from the company I was working for at the time of putting on the *hijab* and she informed me that during that time–totally unbeknownst to me--many of my co-workers had felt and shared a mutual dislike for my new appearance. I was stunned! She continued to give a very detailed account of what had been said about me, and I felt like every word was slicing into me because their accusations and their assumptions had been every fear I had harbored when putting on the *hijab*. I was afraid people would think I was ugly, they did. I was afraid people would think I was 'religious in a bad way', they did. I was afraid people wouldn't like me as much, and they didn't. All this time I had thought of these individuals as a support system for me, all the while they were cruelly isolating me into stereotypes. Being made aware of this a year after the fact hurt however I had moved past all those old worries, so to hear them at this point didn't have the emotional impact that I thought it would. But what if I had been made aware at that time? I was more vulnerable then and if I had known that all my fears were realities, this would have come as a real blow. Maybe I would have quit my job. Maybe I would have found it difficult to trust people again. Maybe I would have become that meek little girl I feared. I realized then I was far from that meek little girl, in fact, I was stronger than I had thought. All I had feared had come to pass and so what? I was still standing. I was still me and what they had said hadn't changed that.

It was at that moment in front of the mall escalators on a random weekday evening that I came to another realization: Allah was my best friend. And I heard people say this in the past and always thought it sounded so hokey but now I knew what it meant. Allah had shielded me from all the gossip; blinded me to what I now see as blatant hypocrisy and opened my eyes to it only when He knew I was ready for it. He had done all this to protect me and help me through a trying time and I had had no idea. Allah, the Lord of the Worlds had had my back. I felt touched, grateful, happy and surprised.

One of the miracles of Allah is that we are able to know things through their opposite and since Allah has no opposite He may feel hidden from us at times. But when He reveals Himself it truly is spectacular. Or perhaps it is better said that when we finally open our hearts to Him, it is spectacular. A promise made and a promise kept: through hardship comes ease.

But this tale is not about *hijab*, it is about youth and what characterizes youth better than heartbreak? Strange for me to say heartbreak since many would think 'wild abandon' or something of a lighter nature would better characterize those tender years, and that may be so but I think heartbreak because your youth is your training ground and boy will you learn! The 'lame' advice that your parents have been giving you for years will finally make sense, as you will learn that you can't trust everyone. You will learn that people can be cruel and two-faced. You will experience moments of isolation, regret and loneliness. And I pray that during these moments your first real step towards Allah will be taken with assurance and resolve. I hope when you feel that sadness that Allah will be the first you turn to and not the phone to call up a friend. Because although times may seem tough, we have learned powerful lessons from real heroes of the past and today I remember a lesson from our hero, prophet Musa.

When Prophet Musa conversed with God, he asked, "Lord, where shall I seek You?"

God answered, "Among the brokenhearted."

Prophet Musa continued, "But, Lord, no heart could be more despairing than mine."

And God replied, "Then I am where you are."[1]

And so He is.

---

[1]. Abu'l-Fayd al-Misri, *"The Kashf al-Mahjub"*

My Love Affair with Egypt

There's something about this place
The busy streets and animated merchants
The honking horns that never quiet down
Streets overflowing with people and noise
Streets overflowing with life

I think I'm in love

But it's the kind of love that's soaked in reality
A non-delusional love
Where all faults are plainly visible to the naked eye
Everything, good and bad, in plain view
There's no escaping the dust and poverty
But there's no escaping the joy either
Laugh lines stroke their faces
As they sit huddled in the doorway
Sipping their afternoon tea in a glass

It's the joy that comes with simplicity
The minimalistic pleasures of a life
That delights in the capacity to enjoy less
And enjoy it so much more

Wedding Day

Nadia sighed as she hit her third red light in a row. Her knuckles tightened around the steering wheel. She glanced at the clock—it was almost four. *Come on*, she thought, staring at the lights. *Don't you know it's my wedding day?*

As she pulled up into her driveway, she thanked God that none of her neighbors were out tending their gardens, or walking their dogs. She didn't want anyone to notice how different she looked today.

Her father greeted her at the door. "Nadia, what took you so long?" he asked, taking the giant cake box out of her hands. "Don't you see?" she asked, motioning to the large bump protruding from beneath her white headscarf. She pulled off the cloth. "My hair!" she exclaimed.

Her father took a step back. "It looks beautiful," he said, a smile playing on his lips. "It's been a long time since I've seen you look this way." Nadia gingerly placed a hand on her newly styled curls. They fell gently from a high ponytail on her head. She stepped towards the mirror. Her father was right. Her hair was lovely. She looked closer, barely recognizing the lined eyes, the pink cheeks and red lips that met her gaze. It had been years since make-up had brushed her skin. She had forgotten its powers.

"Now go and get ready," said her father, as he hurried towards the living room. "Your guests will be here in a few hours."

Nadia watched her father as he went into the kitchen. How different their relationship was compared to a few years ago, she thought. Although they still fell into the occasional argument—her father being a tireless perfectionist who expected nothing less from his children—relations between them had warmed considerably since she began practicing Islam. She held back a wry grin as she remembered the constant fights that marked her teen years. It had started with make-up.

"Green," Nadia murmured to herself as she made her way up the winding stairs. In her room, she stepped over her pearl-colored sandals, past the crème wedding dress that lay on her bed and stopped at the window. "Yes, green," she mused. Her mind had wandered back to the eighth grade, the day she announced to her parents that she would be setting off to school with a new hue above her eyes.

"What?" asked her mother, leaning towards her daughter who sat chomping at her breakfast. "Never," thundered her father as he put down the morning paper.

Nadia would not be put off. "Yes, mom," she said, addressing her usually sympathetic mother. "Today, I'm going to try that green eye shadow that you never use." Her mother squinted at her for a moment, then let out a deep breath. "Okay, fine. I won't stop you but your friends will laugh at you," she warned.

"I don't care what anyone thinks," replied Nadia, thinking that surely her friends had some creative fashion sense and would only support this bold decision. Besides, a shocking green eye shadow was just the type of make-up that one of her favorite teen book characters would likely wear.

"You can't let her wear make-up," said her father, looking angrily at his wife. "This will only be the beginning of our problems." Her mother bit her lip and looked at her daughter. "Don't you think you're too young for make-up?" she asked, trying another tactic. Nadia shook her head stubbornly.

"Fine, she's your daughter," her father said with resignation. It was clear from the defeat etched around his eyes that he didn't have the heart to put his foot down in the face of his daughter's obvious determination. He would wait it out; hoping as he often did that this was just another phase of her teen years – one she would soon grow out of.

When Nadia arrived at school, her best friend ran over to her, laughing. "Nadia," cried Kelly. "What's wrong with your eyes?" Nadia hesitated for a moment. "Well, uh, I've got eye shadow on." Kelly let out a whoop of laughter. "From far away, I thought someone beat you up!" Nadia looked at her friend without saying a word, anger pushing its way up to her throat. "Well, now you see, it's make-up!" she retorted, turning on her heel and heading into school.

Nadia chuckled as she remembered the indignation she felt back then. Too bad the incident hadn't put a damper on her enthusiasm for *Maybelline* and *Cover Girl*. After all, her endless stash of teen magazines cheered her every fashion risk. Her parents watched all this from the sidelines, having no real basis to mount a campaign against what they knew to be 'typical teenage life'; at least that's what they gathered from television. Besides, they themselves had gotten caught up in the glamorous side of Western culture. Her father's only attempt to challenge his daughter's blind imitation of those around her was to ask her to think about how others would react to her behavior. But his question, 'What will people think?' really alluded to members of his cultural community. And Nadia didn't really care what they thought.

"But now, things are so different," she whispered to herself, as she picked up her wedding dress, wondering how she would get it over her elaborate hairdo. *It isn't culture that helps me make decisions, she thought. It's faith.*

She was just squeezing the gown over her head when she heard the doorbell ring. She quickly tugged it down and rushed to the window. Was that her husband-to-be? He and the guests were scheduled to arrive at six o'clock. It wasn't even five.

"Nadia!" Her brother's voice rocketed up the stairs. "Someone is here for you."

Nadia opened her door, catching the muffled sound of a woman's voice. Who could it be, she wondered. She stayed at the top of the stairs, not wanting her father or her brothers to see her in her wedding dress quite yet.

A bright face framed by an opaque headscarf appeared over the staircase.

"Maryam!" she exclaimed happily.

"*Assalamu Allaykum*," replied the elegantly dressed woman, offering the Islamic greeting of peace as they embraced. Nadia ushered her friend into her room.

"Oh, I am so glad you are here," she said, moving her clothes off the bed and motioning Maryam to sit down.

"Well, I had to come early," explained Maryam, her Persian accent accentuating each word. "I wanted to sit with you before this important night." She paused to look at Nadia's dress. "You look so nice," she squealed. For a moment, Nadia almost forgot that Maryam was an older woman. Right then, she seemed no older than twenty-five–the same age as one of her own daughters.

As Maryam talked excitedly, Nadia was reminded of a friend she had long ago. Back in high school, many of her classmates hailed from all parts of the globe. One of them, Shehzada, was from Iran, like Maryam. But that's where the similarities ended.

"Nadia," the tall fifteen-year-old once intoned, her shiny black hair swishing. "We're going bowling today. Why don't you come with us?"

The hallway was brimming with students. The warning bell had just sounded and everyone was heading to class. Except, apparently, Shehzada and her friends.

"Bowling?" repeated Nadia, as she grabbed her English textbook and closed her locker. "Um, I've got class."

"Yeah, so do I," said Shehzada, impatiently. "So what?"

The hallways were already emptying into classrooms where teachers were beginning their lessons. Nadia paused. She could see Shehzada's friends motioning them outside into the beaming April sunshine. Inside, students stared impassively at chalky blackboards. Shrugging away her apprehension, Nadia followed Shehzada to her sister's car.

At the bowling alley, Shehzada soon bored of the endless sound of pins knocking. "Okay guys, this isn't fun," she declared finally, standing with both hands on her hips. The girls twittered and rolled their eyes at Shehzada's typical attitude. "Why don't you go outside," suggested her sister, who was keeping score. Shehzada smiled at the idea. "Yes, outside." She grabbed Nadia by the arm and pulled her along. Nadia didn't have a chance to protest.

Once outside, Shehzada rummaged in the black purse that hung off her thin shoulder. Nadia leaned against the concrete wall facing the barren parking lot. She watched Shehzada wordlessly pull out an unopened pack of cigarettes. She ripped open the plastic wrap and tugged at the foil wrapper. Nadia's eyes widened.

"Okay, wanna try one?" she said, taking out a cigarette and then offering the pack to Nadia.

Nadia nervously tugged at her hair. "I've never smoked," she said, unsure of what to do.

"Oh, it looks easy," laughed Shehzada. She pulled out a silver lighter from her jeans pocket and lit the cigarette. She coughed a few times but was soon smoothly puffing away. Nadia couldn't help but notice how much Shehzada resembled the tall models that graced giant billboards along the roads. They, too, would be casually taking a drag off a long and slender cigarette, looking off into the distance. But instead of the gentle ocean waves or lush green forests as a magnificent vista, a run-down bowling alley served as Shehzada's backdrop. *She looks silly,* thought Nadia. *But I can't lose face.*

She took a cigarette and lit it. The first drags were painful; smoke filled her lungs. She coughed and her eyes watered. "Oh don't worry," said Shehzada. "You'll get used to it."

A few puffs later and Nadia indeed felt like a pro. And despite the ugly taste left in her mouth, she liked the feeling smoking gave her. She felt sophisticated—maybe even as sophisticated as those women in the ads.

Nadia shook her head ruefully at the memory. It had taken her years to quit smoking; much to the chagrin of her parents who eventually tried to help her put an end to her addiction. Her father had even suggested she try a nicotine patch to help her quit—though that was only after he'd gotten over the shock of discovering her unhealthy and embarrassing secret. Patches didn't help, nor lollipops instead of cigarettes. No, what helped her kick the habit was a religious retreat—one she went to without any cigarettes at all. She barely noticed their absence.

"Do we have time to read Qur'an?" Maryam was now asking, as she lit the delicate candles on Nadia's dresser. Nadia nodded.

Maryam's sonorous voice slowly filled the room. Nadia listened quietly, almost forgetting that it was her wedding day. Her body relaxed and she felt a calm descend upon her. She hugged Maryam at the end of the recitation. Maryam gently squeezed her arm.

"*Insha'Allah*, you will be very happy, my dear Nadia."

With her room perched above the front porch, Nadia soon heard her father welcoming their guests. A few of her closest friends had come up to join her and Maryam. They talked loudly, congratulating her and asking for God's blessings. Nadia smiled nervously while they swirled around her.

"Oh you will look so amazing," gushed Safia. "For sure, your husband will be head over heels in love with you," chimed in another friend, Aisha. Nadia wondered if they were right. As she took a last look in the mirror, she couldn't help but feel amazed at the reflection that stared back at her.

Who would have guessed, she thought as she descended the stairs to meet the guests, *that I would be wearing hijab on my wedding day?*

Back in high school, Nadia avoided talking to girls who wore head-scarves. *She must be so religious*, she would think as she passed one of them in the hallway. At the time, there were few Muslims in her school and it became easy for her to forget about religion altogether. Faith was rarely talked about among her circle of friends—they preferred to plan weekends and wardrobes. And while she totally believed in God, she didn't have much time for the rules that came along with that belief, especially after experiencing Islamic camp.

Her parents had wanted to infuse their children with a better understanding of Islam, something they didn't feel well equipped to do. So when the opportunity to send them to an Islamic camp arose, they were thrilled.

"It will be great fun," enthused her mother, helping her pack. Her father settled the whole family into the car to make the three-hour drive to the campgrounds.

After the first hour of being there, Nadia knew fun was out of the question.

"You shouldn't wear bright colors." "You shouldn't laugh out loud." "You shouldn't be seen speaking to boys, even your own brothers." "You shouldn't speak out loud in mixed crowds." It seemed there was no end to the things she shouldn't do.

While Nadia did enjoy spending time with young women her own age, learning about the Qur'an and talking about general principals of Islam, she found the rules at the camp suffocating.

"I don't think this is realistic," she confided to one sister as she grudgingly tugged a pink headscarf over her hair. "Why should I pretend to wear this headscarf?" she asked. "I don't wear it anywhere else!"

The sister looked at her sympathetically. Having attended camp for years, she knew that it seemed tough to newcomers, accustomed to the laissez-faire attitude of their parents. "But this is good practice," she insisted. "Because you should learn how to please Allah."

Nadia remained unconvinced. She felt the camp was too rigid. Upon returning home, she didn't give Islam much more thought. It would be years before it would play any significant role in her life. In the meantime, she would wholeheartedly adopt the ways of the West. Working hard and playing hard without fear of consequences.

That eventually changed.

The 180-degree turn-around began gradually. It kicked into high gear, though, during one summer vacation in Egypt, her parents' country of origin. At first, she basked in the glow of admirers who made their interest plain to her, relishing feeling like a rich and care-free Westerner in her trendy t-shirts and short skirts. The surprise that would flicker across handsome faces when she spoke Arabic, albeit brokenly, was a source of great amusement. But though she was attracted to a familiar Western sub-culture, she couldn't help be drawn to the Islam she was beginning to discover.

Here, Islam was clearly more than a set of dry, strict rules. Those who sincerely practiced it seemed to bring it to life. They lived and breathed their faith. Nadia could see this in the warm relationships between family members and in the caring words of friends and neighbors, and even among strangers. And no matter what went right or wrong, people all around her praised God. Faith was not something reserved for special locations or specific days. No, in Egypt–and other Muslim countries, she suspected–the purpose of life was called out from the rooftops five times a day. She soon found herself answering those calls to prayer as they coaxed her from sleep, interrupted her meals, and bid her good-night after a sun-drenched day.

"Oh, you are Muslim?" a woman asked after Nadia had casually ended a response to a question with *Insha'Allah*, or God willing. It was hardly an uncommon statement. Most Egyptians peppered their conversations with references to God. But perhaps it seemed strange coming from a girl so obviously Western in dress and language. "Yes, *El Hamdullilah*," replied Nadia to the woman's question, thanking God without thinking twice as she reached in her wallet to pay for camera film.

The lady smiled at her as though she had received the greatest news in the world. "*Assalamu Allaykum*," said the woman, bidding Nadia farewell as though she were a cousin or a sister. She didn't say a word about Nadia's uncovered hair, or her bright sleeveless dress.

Slowly, Nadia's heart was awakening to the beauty of Islam. For the first time in her life, Islam was about love, not just about rules; love for the Creator and love for each other. She would regularly squeeze herself into rooms full of covered women, jostling for a place next to them where she would join them in prayer. She'd later photograph the same mosques, unconsciously falling in love with the rich architecture that united so many people within its walls.

Despite the slow spiritual awakening, an invitation arrived that Nadia couldn't resist. A friend of hers had called her up and asked her to join her for a few relaxing days at a popular beach side resort off the coast of the Red Sea. Violetta, an attractive blond woman from Romania, was working at the reception of a five-star hotel and treated like royalty on account of her foreign passport. Unlike the local employees who stayed in crowded staff housing, she had plenty of room in her luxury suite to entertain Nadia. "We will have such a wonderful time!" coaxed Violetta, her throaty voice crackling over the phone lines. *Why not?* Nadia thought. "I'll be there," she replied. She booked a plane ticket and arrived the following weekend.

They spent lazy afternoons on the beach, sunbathing and talking to other foreigners. At night, Violetta would don her hotel uniform and slip behind the reception desk for a few hours of work.

That was when Nadia would set off on the sandy boardwalk, taking in the bright starry skies and rolling waves. It was during one of those strolls that her transformation finally took root.

As she followed her usual path around sunburned crowds of tourists, she found herself becoming unusually irritated with the attention being showered on her by the young local men who idly watched everyone go by. In fact, to her surprise, she felt embarrassed at their compliments, likely tired old lines offered to anyone who would listen. Their heavily accented voices followed her into the brightly lit market. Soon her embarrassment turned to anger and the feminist inside took over.

"How would you like it if your sister or mother were whistled at and looked at in such a way?" she demanded from one group of men who were leaning against a beat-up pick-up truck at the edge of the crowded stalls.

"What?" one of them stammered. "We thought you were Italian," he said motioning to the other women who lounged around the boardwalk flirting with countless Egyptian youth.

Nadia looked into the crowd, noticing the Italian women for the first time. Soap operas were unfolding all around her! And, to make matters worse, the Italian women who giggled in clumsy English were barely dressed! She looked down at her own outfit. Her blue and yellow tank top and fitted white pants seemed so chic in the mirror of the hotel room, she thought bitterly. Now she wished she could disappear. She walked away from the group of men as quickly as she could, not wanting them to look at her anymore.

She was now starting to understand why women were supposed to conceal their beauty when they went out in public. What was that verse she would occasionally read in the Qur'an? Lighting a cigarette, she bumped into a young man with dark hair. A short beard lined his round face.

He noticed her silent tears, her hand shaking as she brought the cigarette to her lips.

"*Maalek*?" What's wrong, he asked.

"They're bothering me," she said weakly, her voice sounding far away as she motioned to the dark shadows.

"Who's bothering you? Show me who they are," he said protectively, as though she were his younger sister. The tears were still falling down her face.

She shook her head. "They are everywhere," she replied, not even looking at him. His forehead furrowed and a slight frown pulled on his face but he didn't say anything. Instead he reached into his shirt pocket and pulled out a small pack of tissues. He handed her the pack. She took it from him, pulling at a tissue. "I want to wear *hijab*," Nadia blurted out suddenly, staring at the air where her words had emerged. The young man's shoulders relaxed. His face broke into a kind smile.

"*Insha'Allah*, you will," he said confidently and started to walk away, as though he knew she would be okay.

"Wait!" she called out after him. He turned around, waiting for her to speak.

"Do you know the verse in the Qur'an where God tells the Prophet that Muslim women should cover up?"

His dark face brightened.

"Yes . . .

"O Prophet, tell your wives and daughters and the believing women to draw their outer garments around them. That is better in order that they may be known and not annoyed..."

When she returned to Canada, Nadia found herself choosing loose shirts over tight ones. Baggy pants over shorts. Calls to prayer echoed in her mind. Boisterous streets surrounded her in her dreams. Faith flickered in her heart.

Nadia soon started talking to her family and friends about Islam.

Her family was pleased with her newfound interest in the faith, though her father secretly hoped his daughter wouldn't wear the Islamic head covering–a symbol of the poor, he thought, and not something anyone among his circle of friends would encourage. As for Nadia's own friends, most of them listened to her thoughtfully, even though they weren't Muslim. They seemed surprised by her fascination with a faith they knew only as strange and even oppressive towards women. How could Nadia–beautiful, intelligent, popular Nadia–fit into that picture? She shattered their misconceptions, armed with new research that had surprised even her. This faith was about worshipping God, she explained. It is a faith in which those who obey God find inner peace while helping to build communities based on truth, equality and justice. A faith, she continued, that discourages actions that could lead to pain and heartache, while promoting and celebrating all that is good and wholesome. She answered their numerous questions with calm and certainty; her confidence was building. Finally, she floated the idea that she, too, wanted to cover up like so many other Muslim women around the world did. And she wanted to know: Would her friends abandon her out of embarrassment at having a Muslim friend? Would they understand that *hijab* was consistent with her feminist beliefs–that people would have to judge her on her character and not on her beauty? Would they shun her for adopting such a visible statement of faith? No, they assured her. *We'll support you all the way.* Her friends made her feel proud to be Canadian.

In fact, surprisingly, it was her father who put up the most resistance. "Who'll hire you?" he asked, noting that she only had one year to go before she completed her undergraduate studies. "It doesn't matter, Dad," she answered with resolve. "I'm not doing this for anyone. This is between me and God." Realizing his daughter's conviction, her father knew he wouldn't be able to discourage her. Besides, he had to admit, Nadia's arguments for wearing the *hijab* were compelling. How could he deny her the right to choose this path? For the first time in her life, she had decided to go against the whims of society, establishing her own identity based on sincere belief. No, he couldn't fall into the cultural trappings that had caught him before when his own wife had wanted to wear *hijab* and he had persuaded her not to bother. This time, he wouldn't withhold his blessing.

And then she did it. The details of the day her life changed course were imprinted on her mind. Nadia had carefully picked up the plain blue scarf she had purchased from an Islamic store downtown and headed downstairs to the hallway mirror of her home. Standing still for a moment, she then brought down the simple cloth over her golden brown hair. Not a strand was visible. She pinned the scarf beneath her chin and tied the ends around her neck. Grabbing her purse and car keys, she stepped outside, mentally fighting the words that hammered her head.

You look stupid; take it off! The seconds felt like hours as she walked towards her car. Her steps were heavy and she stared at the ground, wondering why she couldn't see any mud but felt as though she were sinking.

Nadia fought the temptation to turn around. To run back inside. To rip off this new identity that shifted her world, changed her universe. But she didn't.

Instead, she went to visit her mother. And her mother beamed at the sight of her. *Just as she is beaming today*, thought Nadia, glimpsing her seated among the guests at her wedding.

Nadia took her own seat in the middle of the room. Flowers and people competed for space. Soon, her husband joined her in the seat beside her. The wedding contracts were brought out; the ink barely dry when a curtain came down, separating the men from the women and family members. She went upstairs and removed her *hijab*. Her father came with her.

"Ready?" he asked, handing her a bouquet of flowers.

"Yes, ready," replied Nadia, smoothing her silk scarf over her arms. She took her father's arm shyly. He smiled proudly as they made their way down the staircase.

Her husband stood on the landing. His eyes lit up at the sight of his bride, her long curls nestling around her shoulders. Smiling back at him, Nadia silently thanked God she had made it this far.